Praise for *You Can't Do It!*

Marcus Johns has an incredible ability to see past the obstacles that stand between the pursuer and the dream. Through Marcus's lens, every reader will not only be able to suspend disbelief, but also begin to imagine themselves doing the very things they thought they never could. If you need to be empowered, if you want to believe in yourself again—read this book!

STEVIE AND SAZAN HENDRIX, *The Good Life* podcast

What if you entered a world where your impossible became possible? An environment where you could begin to build confidence in yourself and to see examples of dreams applied with persistence and hard work turn into reality? With a beautiful mixture of wit and brutal honesty, my brother documents his journey of highs and lows and how he's managed to defy the odds in this inspiring read.

ALEXYS AND CODY JOHNS, actress and musician

Marcus has always been a dreamer. He is someone who chases his dreams, whether it's big or small. Being with him for the last five years has changed my life because of the ways he has gotten me to step out of my comfort zone. But even if you just meet Marcus for a brief five minutes, he'll encourage you to go after your dreams and do that one thing you've been too scared to do. This book represents Marcus at his core: loving people, encouraging people, and doing the crazy things no one else thinks you can do.

KRISTIN JOHNS, content creator and CEO of Kristin Made

YOU CAN'T DO IT!

THERE ARE A MILLION REASONS YOU CAN'T—

FIND THE REASON YOU CAN

ZONDERVAN BOOKS

You Can't Do It!

Requests for information should be addressed to:
Zondervan, 3900 Sparks Dr. SE, Grand Rapids, Michigan 49546

Zondervan titles may be purchased in bulk for educational, business, fundraising, or sales promotional use. For information, please email SpecialMarkets@Zondervan.com.

ISBN 978-0-310-35886-2 (audio)

Library of Congress Cataloging-in-Publication Data

Names: Johns, Marcus, 1993– author. | Smucker, Shawn, author.
Title: You can't do it! : there are a million reasons you can't—find the reason you can / Marcus Johns, with Shawn Smucker.
Description: Grand Rapids : Zondervan, 2020. | Includes bibliographical references. | Summary: "No matter what you aim to do, you'll often hear a voice say, 'You can't do it'—either outside or inside you. But maybe that's the perfect reason why you can. With lighthearted insights from his own life, actor and social media star Marcus Johns shifts the perspective on resistance and doubt to change discouraging obstacles into powerful motivators"—Provided by publisher.
Identifiers: LCCN 2020003832 (print) | LCCN 2020003833 (ebook) | ISBN 9780310358831 (hardcover) | ISBN 9780310358848 (ebook)
Subjects: LCSH: Determination (Personality trait) | Achievement motivation. | Christian life.
Classification: LCC BF698.35.D48 J64 2020 (print) | LCC BF698.35.D48 (ebook) | DDC 155.2/32—dc23
LC record available at https://lccn.loc.gov/2020003832
LC ebook record available at https://lccn.loc.gov/2020003833

Cover design: Curt Diepenhorst
Cover photo: Tyler Rowell
Author photo: Jon Sams
Interior design: Denise Froehlich

Printed in the United States of America

---

20 21 22 23 24 /LSC/ 10 9 8 7 6 5 4 3 2 1

To my parents—
for raising me to love God.
To my wife—
for showing me God's love.

Aviation is proof that given the will, we have the capacity to achieve the impossible.

EDWARD VERNON RICKENBACKER

Contents

CHAPTER 1

I Can't Do It

I'm sitting here with a blank page on my computer screen . . .

Okay, now I have one sentence and three dots.

You can see where I'm going with this.

Ugh.

Who am I kidding? I can't write a book.

Especially a book ironically named *You Can't Do It!*—a name that makes the reader think, *Hmmm, let me open up this book and see what this weird guy jumping and pointing has to say about me not being able to do something. He must have the answers, right? I guess I'll see what he has to say.*

And now you are here.

And so am I.

I'm here, sitting at my computer, a year or more before you ever read this in a print book or on some futuristic tablet my mind can't even conceive of. I'm here, just blankly staring at this vast sea of white nothingness on my computer screen, while my blinking cursor of a ship reminds me of the distance I must travel.

Just sitting here, wondering, *How am I ever going to pull this off?*

I am the captain of this ship. I cut ties at the port, and I've set sail with promises of treasure for myself, as well as for a book publisher who thought it was a good idea to trust me to do this with nothing more than a map . . . that I drew.

And by map, I mean a crumpled piece of paper that had the name of twelve different chapters I'm supposed to write.

I think you get the point.

I can't do this.

And also, this sailing metaphor is making me seasick.

Truly, if anyone ever reads this message floating in a bottle (or on a bookshelf), just know that these were the first words I wrote, unedited, when taking on this whale of a task.

Okay, now I'm done with the sailing metaphors.

I guess the point of this is to say you or I will never completely escape the feelings of self-doubt, and "You Can't Do It" will always follow you. But if we'll pursue our goal, just one word at a time, we can finish page 1.

And if we can write one page, we can write a book.

So, what new endeavor are you setting out on?

Writing a book?

Making a movie?

Starting a new business?

Becoming an influencer?

Getting married?

Being a parent?

Creating a musical?

Whatever it is you're thinking about doing, guess what? Someone is bound to tell you that you can't do it. Complete strangers, friends, even family members will at some point question your ability, your talent, your work ethic, and sometimes your sanity.

"Are you sure this is a good idea?"

That's usually the spin they'll put on it, but what they're really trying to say, in as nice a way as possible, is, "You can't do this. I wouldn't even try."

Sometimes the people closest to you are the ones who have the least confidence in you.

Maybe those around you think they know who you are better than you do. Maybe they think they're genuinely going to save you from some kind of disappointment down the road. They don't want to see you get hurt, so they try to keep you from going after your dreams.

There's a lot of negativity in the world—some of it just happens, but some of it is intentional. And let me tell you, I don't judge anyone for giving in to the negative voices, because those voices are loud and persistent, and sometimes they . . .

Just.

Won't.

Stop.

But let me tell you this.

You don't have to listen to them. You can get past them. You can do what you're setting out to do. Just be prepared. Because there are a ton of people out there who will try to convince you that it can't be done.

But before we get into dealing with other people who are telling you it can't be done, there's one person we have to talk about first. Of all the people in the world who will doubt you, it's this one person whose doubt has the power to absolutely crush you. If you can't move beyond this particular person's doubt, you'll get nowhere.

You know who I'm talking about.

Not your mom or your dad or your best friend.

Not that troll on social media.

I'm talking about you.

If you're reading this book, you know what it's like. And

if not, then just read page 1. I modeled it for you. You're welcome.

You want to create something new, make a big splash, follow your dreams?

There's something out there you want to do or be, and for some crazy reason, you think you might actually be able to do it. But whenever you start going in that direction, whenever you think about taking the first step, the voices start up—the ones that try to keep you from even getting started.

Do any of these sound familiar to you?

There are people way more influential than you. Let them do it.

You're too young. No one cares about what you have to say.

You're too old. You're irrelevant now.

Someone's already done that. Everyone will think you're unoriginal.

You don't have the résumé for this project. You definitely need more experience.

You can't. You just don't have the skill.

The people who will tell you you can't do it are everywhere.

But they're not your biggest problem.

The First Time I Chased a Dream

When I was young, I wasn't into acting or singing or anything else in the arts. Not when I was little anyway. I just wanted to play soccer and be a kid, do all the boy stuff like climbing trees and running around and wrestling with my older brother, Cody. But Cody? He actually got into acting at a young age. In fact, he went the homeschool route specifically so he'd have time to go to auditions, take special classes, and focus completely on trying to land roles.

He loved it.

So early on, I lived with someone who was chasing their dreams.

My parents wanted me to get into acting too, but they never brought it up in a pushy way. I think they saw in my personality that I had natural raw talent, but when I didn't show much interest, they let me get on with my life and do the things I wanted to do. They were smart not to force me in that direction. That's exactly what would have caused me to resist it.

But all of this changed one day when I was ten years old. Cody had an audition for a movie role that his agent recommended he try out for. When he showed up, the casting director was surprised—it turned out they were looking for someone younger.

Much younger.

Someone my age.

"Marcus," my mom said after Cody told her what had happened, "why don't you just give it a shot? It's a big opportunity, and movies like this don't come to Florida very often. You may as well try out for the part."

Thinking back, I now realize why I never wanted to act. It wasn't because I didn't like the idea, or because I thought it wasn't going to be fun. It was because that was *my brother's thing*. I was constantly being compared to Cody, and I took any chance to show I was different.

So I told myself I couldn't act.

The funny thing is that it was all in my head. No one was comparing me; it was just my own inner, doubting voice telling me I couldn't do the same thing as my older brother. He was the actor, not me. He was the one trying out for movie roles, not me.

If it weren't for Cody encouraging me and saying I really should try out, I probably wouldn't have done it. But the fact that this opportunity was only for me and we weren't competing for the role made me feel comfortable enough to try.

I remember practicing my lines with my mom, just the two of us reading back and forth. It was the first time I had ever done anything like that, but I had seen my brother do it countless times, so I tried to mimic him. Almost immediately I realized I was good at memorizing my lines quickly, even though I had always thought that would be the hardest part. I remember having this overwhelming sensation that acting might be something I enjoyed, something I might be very good at. Before I tried it, I thought it would maybe feel like homework, but soon I realized I could just have fun and play. I had a big personality, even when I was ten years old, so it came fairly naturally to me.

My mom and I drove down to Miami later that week, and I walked into the room. I couldn't stop thinking, *This is my first audition. This is my first audition.* But even in the moment, I wasn't exactly nervous, at least not in any negative sense. I was excited. I was amped-up. But I didn't feel like I had anything to lose. If I didn't get the part, I'd just go back to being my zany, off-the-wall self, and Cody could do all the formal acting stuff.

At least that's what I kept telling myself.

But then I started thinking, *What if I did get the part? What would that mean?*

Could I measure up to Cody?

Maybe I would be let down. Or let everyone else down.

I wasn't sure.

"Okay," the manager said to me as I stood there, my mind racing. "Let's read the lines. Ready, Marcus?"

I did it, and when we finished, I looked up. I felt like it had gone really well, but it was my first time reading lines with a real live person from the movies. I had no idea how I'd done or what they thought.

"That was incredible!" the manager exclaimed. "That was so good. So good." He kept gushing, and I felt this intense feeling. It was like happiness, but with the volume turned up. I was actually good at it! His affirmation was an incredible feeling.

"I can tell you right now that we'd like you to do a callback in Tampa with the main casting director. I'll schedule things with your mother. I'm looking forward to this, Marcus." He nodded, and I walked out.

Or maybe I floated out—I'm not sure.

It might have been a few days later or it might have been a week, but we drove to Tampa, just my mom and I, and that felt like a really big deal because it was a two-and-a-half-hour drive and I knew, going there, that I had a real shot to land the role. The same phrase kept rolling through my brain: *I might be in a movie, I might be in a movie, I might be in a movie.* But I knew nothing was for sure.

We pulled into this commercial area, a kind of business park, and we went inside. Sitting in the waiting room with me was one other kid. It was completely quiet, and eventually someone came out and got him, and he went in first. Then he came out and left. I watched him closely to see if I could tell anything about how it had gone for him, but I couldn't get a sense either way. Unlike the first tryout, I definitely felt some nerves this time around, but even there, at my very first callback, I wasn't feeling anxious. It was that excited kind of nervousness—I was eager to perform, looking forward to showing them what I could do.

The person who had taken the first boy in came back out.

"Okay, Marcus. We're ready for you."

I followed them into the audition room. I wondered if there might be a bigger audience, but it was mostly empty. One was the director of the movie, and I recognized him right away. It might have made me even more nervous, but he was so kind that he put me completely at ease.

"Okay, Marcus, let's do a scene, bud."

Five ~~Simple~~ Ways to Overcome Self-Doubt

It's easy to look at people who seem popular and talented and think that, surely, they never struggle with self-doubt.

They're so successful.

They're so talented.

They're so naturally gifted.

We watch people in the movies or on TV and think their life is one unending stream of self-confidence and certainty. With that kind of success, with that level of fame and popularity, what reason could they possibly have to doubt themselves?

You would be surprised.

Everyone experiences self-doubt.

And everyone has to figure out a way to fight their way through it.

Just because you experience self-doubt doesn't mean you have to act on it. Just because the voices in your head are telling you you're not good enough doesn't mean you have to listen to them. Everyone who does anything goes through periods where they want to give up, think they can't cut it, or conclude maybe it's time to go work in a laundromat. Or study political science. Or deliver newspapers.

I only mention those because I've done all of them at some point in my life.

I did those things because I didn't know what I was doing.

But there are a few things I've learned from my many battles with self-doubt. These are a few things I've tried that have helped:

Give yourself permission to break out of the box. We all do it. We all create these boxes around what it is we're good at. I thought I might be good at acting, but (for the reasons I mentioned) I didn't want to give it a try. Yet sometimes the best way to battle through self-doubt is to try something new. Try a fresh approach to the stuff you're good at, or try something completely different. If you're a classical piano player, try playing pop music. If you love to act in modern plays, try Shakespeare. When you break out of the box, there's less pressure, because you're trying something you're not supposed to be good at. And you might even find something new that you love.

Sometimes other people put you in a box because you've had some success, and they think that's the only thing you can do. Most people find it hard to believe that just because you've done well at one thing doesn't mean you want to keep doing that same thing for the rest of your life. I've experienced that so much, and I've heard all the reasons people will give.

But don't be afraid to try something different. It may be just what you need to quiet the self-doubt and find something you truly love.

Fall in love with the work. The only way you're going to get better at something (and getting better is a great way to get rid of self-doubt) is by working at it. Really hard. A lot.

Sure, that thing you love to do starts out as a dream, but unless you let that dream translate into consistent, disciplined effort, you're not going anywhere. So figure out what it is about this thing that you love, and then work at it. And find the interesting parts of it to fall in love with, so the work becomes rewarding on its own—not just rewarding *after* the work.

Once I realized I loved to act, I worked at it. I practiced all the time. I paid attention to how talented actors did their work. I wanted to learn.

I didn't love every bit of it. But there was enough that I found to love, and it pushed me forward. This is one of the best ways to quiet self-doubt—and when you get more into whatever it is, you will begin to fall in love with the work.

Stop comparing yourself to others. Listen, if there's one thing that will stop you dead in your tracks, it's comparison. Comparing yourself to someone else, someone who's in a completely different reality, completely different situation, with completely different talents, and stacking yourself up against them?

It's a completely worthless exercise.

Don't do it.

I know how hard it can be NOT to compare yourself to others. When I was in the middle of producing my musical (more on that later), all these incredible singers were coming in and auditioning for parts, and I was sitting there listening to them and knowing that, as the lead, my voice would be directly compared to them once the show started. I didn't think I sounded as talented as they did. I was sure the audience would hear us singing together and immediately make judgments about my singing. I even imagined the comments that would show up online once we shared the musical with the internet.

The funny thing is, when the musical finally happened, the difference between my voice and the other singers didn't matter at all. I realized during one of our first practices that my unique voice was what made me special.

That was me.

No one else could do that.

The same is true for you—no one can be you. No one has the unique talents, personality, and approach that you have. No one can create that one-of-a-kind thing that you're working on.

So stop comparing yourself to others, and give yourself permission to be you. If you do this, you'll start quieting that voice of self-doubt.

Put stuff out there. One of the biggest contributors to self-doubt is perfectionism, because you think that if something isn't perfect, you can't release it to the world. You write something, but when you read back through it, it's not what you expected so you delete it. Or you paint something, or you take a photo, or you make a video for YouTube, and when it doesn't quite measure up, you shake your head, disappointed with yourself, and stick it in a file folder. Or you delete it.

Go ahead—ask me how I know. The thing about perfectionism is that it's not all bad—it's good to have high expectations of your work. It's good to demand the best of yourself. It's good to keep reworking things until they're as good as they can be.

But you know the deal—for the good stuff to rise to the top, eventually you have to put it out there.

If you've created art, something that is actually great,

people will follow you and ask for more. Do good work, but after you do, don't sit on it. Get into the habit of finishing your work and putting it out there.

Cultivate your own version of greatness . . . with blinders on. As you're giving yourself permission to try new things, as you're falling in love with working hard, and as you're putting your stuff out there without comparing to others . . . also keep your blinders on. Self-doubt is going to try to draw your attention to all of the other interesting, popular things in the world and tell you the ways your stuff is not as good as that stuff. Remember our old friend Comparison?

Don't listen.

Don't pay attention.

Don't follow the trends, because if you follow a trend, you become a trend, and you know what trends do?

They come and go.

You don't want to come and go as quickly as the next trend.

Instead, keep pursing your own unique version of greatness. Keep your eyes on your goal. And keep your blinders on about everyone else's work.

Becoming an Actor, and Then Forgetting I Was an Actor

At that first callback in Tampa, I went through the lines I had rehearsed, giving it my absolute best. And I loved it, every bit of it—the experience, the environment, the electricity in the air. As soon as I finished, the other people in the room looked at each other, nodded, and looked back at me.

"Okay, Marcus. Great job. You've got the part. When can you start?"

What! This massive rush of adrenaline raced through me, and I couldn't stop smiling. I got the part! I couldn't believe it. I walked out to the waiting room, and they told my mom.

"He's got the part. He's going to be in the movie."

It felt amazing. Best of all, I didn't have to go home and wonder for weeks what their decision would be. I didn't have to live with that uncertainty. Whenever I'm involved in casting now, if I know someone is going to get the part, I try to tell them right there, on the spot. It's pretty rare, but it's such an incredible moment when you can get that.

After we finalized plans with them, my mom and I walked out of the building. It was right next to a convention center, and there was a large harbor we walked along, and I remember thinking over and over, *I'm going to be in a movie!* Back at the car, Mom and I called the rest of the family and gave them the news, and everyone was clapping and cheering in the background. It was one of the best moments of my life up to that point. It was so surreal.

I *could* do it.

I *could* act!

After that day, something shifted in me—I became the actor kid. And I liked it. I really liked it. It became my new identity. I attended a performing arts middle school and tried out for as many theatrical parts as I could. I was passionate about it, and I worked really hard. That first victory gave me a confidence boost, and I set out in that new direction, excited to see what would happen.

But guess what happened next?

Hint: it involves self-doubt.

I've recently noticed that my own self-doubt is pretty predictable—even after I'm successful at something, if enough time passes, I'll downplay it. It's like time passes, and anything I've been good at in the past just disappears. It's like it never even happened.

Maybe you do that too. Maybe you have selective memory like I do.

We end up telling ourselves all kinds of crazy stuff.

Well, it wasn't that big of a deal. I mean, a lot of people probably could have done it.

It was so long ago—maybe I'm not that good anymore.

I started to doubt the success, minimizing my accomplishment, and soon I convinced myself it was only luck. I landed that movie part because my brother was working hard in the business and the timing was right and I was there.

I started picking up new hobbies, new interests.

I lost my focus on acting.

In other words, my self-doubt kicked in, and I drifted away from an area where I had been successful.

Only a few short years after that first movie role, by the time I was staring down my freshman year of high school, I decided to check out of the performing arts school. I walked away from acting and singing. I got interested in politics and discovered it was entertaining to talk about current topics and debate other students. I decided that once I got to college, I'd study political science.

Is that surprising? From acting in a Hollywood movie at ten to . . . political science. Kind of crazy, right? One moment, I was a success at this thing that tons of people want to do, really going after it, and the next moment I just walked away from it because I didn't think it would work out.

I let my self-doubt change the entire direction of my life.

But then someone else came along, a different voice—one that put me back on track.

And Then . . . Vine

I remember a specific moment about halfway through my senior year of high school, long after I had buried my hopes and dreams of acting and singing and performing. I was backstage at my high school, and I can't even remember how I ended up back there, but for some reason I started playing the piano and singing a song my brother, Cody, had taught me. I wasn't paying attention to anything else around me. I was just in the moment, totally enjoying myself.

"Whoa, Marcus!" a voice said, and I quickly stopped and looked around. I hadn't realized anyone else was watching. Turns out, it was CJ Wetzler, one of my brother's friends. He had a big smile, and I kind of thought he was going to make fun of me.

"You sound amazing!" he said. I tried to laugh off the compliment, but he kept going. "I'm serious. You should sing more often. I didn't know you were so talented."

His words woke something up inside me, something that had been asleep for a long time. I thought to myself, *He's right. I am actually good at this.*

A pause, and then, *Why don't I do this more often?*

Why did I stop acting? I couldn't even remember.

My self-doubt had tried to keep me from doing the things I loved, but one word of encouragement was all it took to get me back in the game. Later that year, because CJ had encouraged me, I entered and won a talent show at the school. And in our high school, this thing was a huge deal. That victory gave me even more courage, enough to try out for the spring musical during my senior year.

And I landed the lead part.

I had rediscovered my passion for performing. I

remembered that, yes, I was good at it, and it was something I wanted to work hard at. When I graduated from high school, I went back to my talent agent's office and told them I wanted to start acting again. I wanted to update my profile and see if I could make it as an actor.

"Okay, well, what are you into now?" my agent asked as we were catching up.

"I started singing again," I mentioned. "And I love to act."

"Anything else?" he asked.

"Oh, yeah," I added as an afterthought. "Right now, I'm really into playing the drums too."

He looked at me with a strange look on his face.

"It just so happens I know of a movie that's looking for a young man your age who can play the drums. I think you should audition."

And that's how I ended up in *Rock of Ages* with Tom Cruise and Julianne Hough. It was all because my brother's friend encouraged me when I was playing a piano backstage, and I moved beyond my self-doubt.

Never forget the power your encouraging words might have for someone.

And never let self-doubt keep you from going for it.

As you've probably experienced, fighting self-doubt isn't a one-and-done kind of thing. The negative voices are always waiting for an opportunity to come to the surface and kick your butt. Sometimes rejection or failure will make space for them to start talking again, or it may just be long periods of time between successes. Either way, self-doubt is something anyone who's honest has to battle, not just once, but pretty frequently.

Soon after *Rock of Ages*, I decided I wanted to make videos, so I bought this cheapo camera and started posting stuff to YouTube, trying to grow some internet following. I knew other people who had done it, and I figured I'd give it a shot. It couldn't be that hard, right? Besides, I was funny and had some new ideas.

But self-doubt started bogging me down again, even after I had landed a second role in a movie. It just kept coming back around.

You'll never be able to make videos that people want to watch, it said.

YouTube is way too mature and established in the market—new people like you can't break in.

Are you sure you have the talent that some of these other successful YouTubers have?

You should probably just go back to mowing lawns and working in a laundromat.

And, yes, that's what I did. Yet again, I listened to those voices of self-doubt, stopped making YouTube videos soon after I started, and went back to mowing lawns and working in a laundromat to make some money. I took up off-roading, learned how to be a mechanic, and spent a lot of time working on my truck. I distracted myself from the dreams that seemed unattainable by doing other things I enjoyed.

If you would have known me during that time of my life, at eighteen years old, you might have thought that self-doubt had won, that I'd given up and would never go back to working hard at pursuing my passion again.

That's what self-doubt can do.

Thankfully, that wasn't the end of the story.

While I was at the laundromat, I heard about a new platform that had exploded onto the scene: Vine.

I still remember the day my brother sent me a video he had seen.

"Dude, this is a fun app," he said. "You should definitely download it."

I checked it out.

I was hooked.

For those of you who missed this bit of the history of the internet, Vine was a video-hosting service where users could share six-second videos that looped. It started in June 2012. Three years later it had a reported 200 million users.[1] No one had any idea where it was headed. I just thought it was fun. And the more Vines I posted, the more I realized something—I was pretty good at it.

My very first Vine was a reflection of my thinking I had missed the boat again. I made fun of that self-doubt still plaguing me. I wore a grandma's wig, glasses, and a polka-dot dress. I leaned on a cane. And I looked into the camera and said in a shaky voice, "I'm just now on Vine." I was joking, but it was my honest feeling. I thought I might be late to the game . . . just like I'd suspected about YouTube.

But the work was invigorating and I couldn't give up, even though it was a slow grind in the beginning. It was like inventing this entirely new form of entertainment, telling a story in six seconds. Six seconds! Had anyone ever tried this before? And it was a blast, feeling I was at the forefront of an innovative movement. Every day, I tried something new. Every day, I studied what was working for others.

I fell in love with the work.

I was putting stuff out there.

I was breaking out of the box.

And, yes, I may have become a bit obsessed.

I remember seeing this one guy who was pretty well known on Vine, and I realized he had five thousand followers. Only five thousand! I thought I could do that pretty easily, so that became my goal. Could I somehow get that many people to follow me?

Then came a series of Vines when everything started changing for me.

I climbed up to the second story of a building and jumped onto a palm tree. And then, like a total idiot, I slid down. If you got a certain number of likes per minute, the almighty algorithms placed your video on Vine's "Pop Now" page (Vine's equivalent of trending). I got a good reaction, and I did a few more crazy stunts. I was coming up with a character, and I'd say (or shout or scream), "Sometimes you just don't care!"

It was humor at my own expense.

And people seemed to love it.

I hit my goal of five thousand Vine followers . . . and flew right past it. By 2016, I had more than 6.5 million followers.

I couldn't believe it.

6.5 million.

Crazy, right?

And all because I fought the voices of self-doubt with the strongest weapon I had—mockery.

So let me ask you: What's your strongest weapon against your own self-doubt? What goals should you be reaching for beyond the voice inside your head—the voice that's telling you it can't be done?

You Can't Write a Book

Remember how I started this chapter?

The voices of self-doubt in my head told me I couldn't write this book. And they're always coming up with some pretty convincing arguments.

You've never done this before—what makes you think you can write a book?

What about your life could ever warrant the writing of a book?

There are people way bigger than you who have a harder story, who have walked a harder path. Maybe they should write a book instead?

Why do you think your story is worth telling?

Not bad, Self-Doubt. Not bad at all.

Nice try.

The thing is, the challenge of writing this book both excites and terrifies me, which is precisely the combination that makes me want to keep going, keep trying. When I auditioned for that movie in elementary school, or when I competed in the talent contest or auditioned for the lead role in my high school's musical, or when I jumped off a second-story building and slid down a palm tree, every single one of those things excited and terrified me, both at the same time. When I feel those things, it's become clear I should lean in, keep trying, embrace the fear and the excitement, and give it my all. When I'm feeling those things, it's time to stop listening to the voices of self-doubt.

Besides, my story is as valid as anyone else's.

Why not me? Why not my story?

Do you believe that?

Think about it—what is something in your life that excites and terrifies you? What's something that fills you with both fear and anticipation?

Maybe that's the direction you should be going, regardless of what the voices of self-doubt are telling you. Maybe it's time to break out of your box, fall in love with the hard work, stop comparing yourself to others, put your stuff out there, and pursue your own version of greatness . . . and forget all else.

Why not you? That's the question to ask your self-doubt: *Why not me?*

And of course, you're not the only person in the world who will tell you it can't be done. Others will jump on that bandwagon, even after you've stopped listening to your self-doubt.

So we need to move on: What are you going to do when it's not you being negative anymore?

What are you going to do when someone else is saying, "You can't do it"?

CHAPTER 2

That Time I Quit

I was excited and terrified.

I had created one of the most-followed accounts on Vine, gaining upwards of sixty thousand followers a day for nearly two months. But with that success came the pressure of having to one-up myself every single day.

A better video, and more likes.

Every day.

Somehow during that time, I kept it up, throwing new videos out there without any second-guessing, and for a time it felt like every video idea was a banger. Not only did I feel this way—I had the numbers to back it up.

During the summer of 2013, nearly every video I posted charted at number one on "Pop Now," a simple algorithm of whose videos received the most amount of likes per minute. And no one could touch me. It was a fun season of life, feeling like everything was going my way. But most of all, the feeling of being creative and productive while overcoming the voices of self-doubt was the most rewarding part of it all. The fact that I was operating on pure instincts, and my instincts were right every time.

I remember the peak of it all—or at least the beginning of the peak. It was a huge landmark that appeared on my Vine horizon. I was closing in on one million followers.

And no one on the app had reached it yet. As I got closer to achieving that, I knew I wanted to mark the occasion by doing something special. Something different. Something that would get everyone's attention while also thanking people for joining me on the journey. I thought about it for a while, and figured there were many different avenues I could take.

Maybe I'd base it on the kinds of videos I was already creating, somehow coming up with a compilation of all my characters or ideas?

No, that wasn't good enough. Bigger, something new.

I could try something risky, something that was nearly death-defying.

What I had in mind, while possible and jaw-dropping, just didn't have that victorious ring I was looking for.

I could do something embarrassing. But I did that all the time.

Maybe I could pull in someone famous to mark the occasion with me, another internet celebrity or movie star? I had some ideas to pull that off.

No. That didn't feel right either.

What could I do in six seconds that would be an appropriate celebration?

Something fantastic—new and different. Something of epic proportions. Dare I say, game-changing?

And then it came to me.

What if I could change the game?

I knew if I could hack into Vine's system, figure out their video specifications, and upload an *edited* video, something you weren't able to do using their standard platform, that would be truly special. Something that would grab everyone's attention and conceivably achieve the impossible.

They would all say, "How did he do that?"

Yes. This impossible idea started getting traction in my mind.

But I know what you're probably wondering by now.

Am I a hacker by trade, able to rearrange code and break into online bank vaults? No.

Am I some kind of a computer wizard? No.

Am I stubborn and curious enough to keep trying something until I find a solution?

Yes.

Yes, I am.

Before I get too far into sharing this story, I should explain that when Vine started, they went to great lengths to make sure that all of the six-second videos that people uploaded were recorded live and unedited. The platform was set up in such a way that it didn't allow for edited videos to be posted—you simply opened the app, turned on the camera, and recorded exclusively by holding your finger on the screen. There was no way around this. But I was determined to figure out how to shoot a video, edit it on my computer, and then somehow upload it to my Vine account, all in time to celebrate my one millionth follower. It would be my magnum opus of sorts. And the day was just around the corner.

I didn't have much time.

It was a long and complicated process. I started by using a desktop phone reader that allowed me to read and manipulate the input file, find the temp file stored in the app just before uploading and replace it with a different file (with the same name), tricking the app into uploading the new file I had edited.

But you couldn't just substitute any old video in

there—you had to upload one that had the exact same specs as Vine's standard video recorder. The problem was, nobody knew what that was. Those specifications weren't public knowledge, so I ended up painstakingly attempting every possible combination of encoding specifications via trial and error. Everything from format, frame rate, codec, file name, mixdown, hertz, sample rate, and bit rate—right on down to the decimal point.

I know, "Blah blah blah." It's technical. Let me put it this way: I had to create a video that would look and sound exactly like a normal Vine video or it would get spotted by some algorithm and deleted automatically.

So I made a dummy Vine account to test my theory. Once I thought I had it figured out, I posted an edited video, a simple one, just to see what would happen.

Upload fail.

Over and over, it wouldn't take. I was way off the mark. But I was way too determined to quit.

Days went by, and then I hit the mother lode.

Ah! That's it! Change the original source file before attempting. The system is red-flagging the duplicates, which in the Vine world would be totally impossible.

Like a dummy I was trying to upload the same exact file over and over with just different specs, but the algorithm knew all along. At least that was my theory! So from now on, for every attempt I'd need to record, edit, and export a new test video. This would take me even more time, but I kept trying.

I changed the video file, and I finally got a successful upload!

And in a flash, it was deleted off my home page.

I was getting close. So I tried again. And again. And

again. I got closer to figuring it out with each attempt because the videos would stay up longer and longer. Five seconds. Ten seconds.

Wait, was it staying up?

No way!

But then I refreshed, and the video disappeared. I knew if I could figure out the specs, I might be able to get it to stay. I became obsessed with trying to figure it out—before my one millionth follower came on board. But time was running out. I had planned on having two weeks to pull this off. It turns out I only had three days.

Of course, this was a good problem to have.

One day before my projected million mark, I posted a generic video for the bajillionth time, and this time the video stayed up. Even after I refreshed, IT STAYED.

I didn't believe it.

Were my eyes playing tricks on me?

I refreshed again, and I watched the little loading wheel spin. It was still up!

I closed the app. Opened it.

It was still up.

IT WAS STILL UP!

Dude, I had just hacked the mainframe. Are you kidding me?

I couldn't believe it. I finally had the magic numbers: r480 kbps500 sr44.1 br128.

I was flying under their radar—I knew the specs. I was the only regular user in the world who could now post edited videos to my Vine account.

I knew that after I posted this video, people were going to absolutely lose their minds. Some people would simply enjoy the edited video. But some people would freak out because I had broken in and they'd be desperate to know how I did it. And I had just hit a million followers.

A million followers?

No Viner had done it before. And I knew people would question how this kid had done it, how he'd waited to drop this bomb until the day he hit a mil. *Get outta here!*

At least that's how I played it in my mind.

Either way, the plan was in full effect.

The next day, I posted an obviously edited video in celebration of reaching that milestone. It was shot in slow motion in widescreen, clearly shot on a nice camera (not the usual compressed phone footage like every other video on Vine), and the audio had legit 808 bass. (Vines were also usually characterized by poor music or sound quality because you would have to record any music or effects you wanted in playback on another speaker.)

And I was right. It blew people's minds. Everyone wondered how I had done it. It looked and sounded amazing, and all of my forecasts came true. People freaked out, and for all the reasons I thought they would. The whole platform was buzzing about the video, everyone wondering how in the world I had been able to get this edited clip onto Vine's platform. I didn't say anything. I didn't acknowledge it was edited. I simply thanked everyone for their well-wishes.

But on my side of the screen? I couldn't stop grinning. I had done it. I had figured it out.

Three hours later, Vine deleted it.

Seriously.

Now, to be clear, I'd suspected this might happen. What I had done wasn't strictly against the rules—there were no specific regulations about uploading edited videos—but I guessed it could be against the spirit of what they were trying to do. Maybe they didn't expect anyone to spend the time to figure it out. Whatever the case, once I realized the video was deleted, I posted another one, along with a caption: "Wow, guys. Why would you delete my millionth-follower video?"

That video made a huge splash, and it got even bigger than the one before. Some people were upset with Vine for taking it off; others kept asking how I had done it. Some people were glad it had been deleted and shared their opinion that posting edited videos was cheating the system.

In the moment, all I wanted to know was what Vine had thought about it. Were they furious? Did they chuckle? Were they going to ban me?

I didn't have to wait long to find out. Later that day, someone got in touch with me.

"Marcus, check your Twitter DMs," they said. "The folks at Vine are trying to reach you."

Vine? Trying to reach me?

That made the whole thing even more bizarre, because the Vine executives were these mysterious people in a high castle. They never reached out to anyone. They never took anyone's messages. They were like ghosts, even to those of us who were some of the top creators. There was a solid wall between Vine and those of us who made it a success, and I'd learned early on not to try to see behind the curtain.

And now they were trying to reach me?

The message I received on Twitter went something like this. "Marcus, you obviously posted an edited video, which is why we deleted it, but to be honest, we're not sure what to do with this because it had good success. We didn't build this into our system, and we're still not sure if we want people to upload edited videos. We'll put yours back up, but only this once. Just don't do it again, or we will be forced to delete them."

That was it.

No big deal, more like a slap on the wrist.

I sighed with relief—I had been able to post an awesome video to celebrate my one millionth follower. I hadn't gotten into trouble, and they were even going to leave it up. Also, I got to talk to the men in the high tower.

Crazy.

After that, I taught a few friends how to post edited videos, showing them the exact specs needed to evade the system's red flags, but their videos always got deleted. Vine had decided to crack down on the practice. And for a little while, we all thought edited videos had come and gone in the span of one day. I was proud I had done it, and I thought it was too bad they were limiting it—there were so many cool things you could do in six seconds if you had the opportunity to edit—but I had my fun. No worries. I figured we'd all move on, and Vine would return to the normal spontaneously shot videos it was known for.

Well, a couple of weeks passed, and I saw another edited video show up on Vine—I could tell, and it seemed everyone else could tell it was edited too. Turns out, a company had seen my video, explored doing it themselves, and figured it out. They started posting edited videos in their sponsored posts and advertisements.

And their videos weren't getting deleted.

Then other people started to upload edits and get a good number of likes. Enough to where I knew Vine must be seeing it and still weren't doing anything about it.

Now I was really curious. But I figured I should at least try to get back into it again. So I did. I started posting edited videos, and apparently the powers that be at Vine didn't care anymore. After all, they had my DM and could have messaged me at any point. But they let them go, and my stuff was really blowing up—especially the edited ones. I could do all kinds of creative shots and effects in edited videos that no one else was doing. I was hitting a whole new level of creativity, and I had a full leg up on the competition.

And then came the fallout.

A group of Viners I considered to be friends saw how quickly my following was growing and that I had a tool no one else had access to, and maybe because they were so jealous, they started subtweeting me and trash-talking. There were three of them, and they came against me hard, claiming I was lame, cheating the system, doing things they would never do because edited videos weren't "pure" and weren't "real Vines."

You know. All that super important stuff serious people care about when they notice you're doing something they didn't think of first or just plain don't know how to do.

But for some reason, I was sincerely torn.

People had said it couldn't be done, and I had done it. But now some top Viners were saying it *shouldn't* be done—that's what got me. Like I was a cheater. I didn't want to be seen as a cheater or get ostracized from the community.

So should I keep posting edited videos, or should I back off? Apart from a couple salty peers, millions of people seemed to love them. And the Vine guys never deleted my videos or messaged me.

I didn't know what to do.

Who Do You Listen To?

There I was, getting this pressure from top Viners (granted, on the internet) to stop posting my edited videos, and these people had been my friends. Or at least, they'd been friendly. Maybe they weren't real friends. Suddenly I felt self-conscious about some of the things they were saying about me—insisting I was intentionally cheating the system, that I was someone who couldn't succeed without skirting the rules, someone who got his success because of an unfair advantage.

On the other hand, my brother, who is the voice of reason, told me to keep going.

"These people aren't your friends, man," he kept telling me. "Don't listen to them. You reached a million followers and became the most followed person before you even posted an edited Vine. They're just jealous they didn't think of it first. Don't stop now. You're really hitting your stride!"

He was right. I was averaging sixty thousand new followers each day.

I wish I would have listened to him.

I wish I would have remembered that he has always had my best in mind. But you know what I did? I stopped making edited videos. It was one of those moments when I was told I couldn't do it, and I listened, and it sent me into a huge slump on Vine. It really hurt my growth. My creativity took a hit because for a while I felt like I was lost, and the edited videos that had been surging in popularity were gone. Had I continued putting up those videos, I probably would have easily ridden it to an extra million followers plus.

But I listened to the voices, and I stopped.

None of us want to be told we can't do it. No one wants others to look at them and basically tell them they're not good enough or smart enough or talented enough to do what they want to do. No one wants to be on the end of that kind of "You can't do it."

But the thing is—and this can be hard to hear—sometimes those voices are right. We need to be honest that there are times when someone tells you you can't do it that they're doing you a favor. That "thing" you want to do isn't right for you for some reason—and there may be good reasons. Maybe you're not ready or you'll hurt someone. Maybe you'll potentially hurt yourself and they're keeping you from embarrassing yourself. How many of those singers on *American Idol* could have benefited from someone close to them saying, "Listen. Don't do it."

So how do you know the difference? How can you tell when you need to listen to someone who's telling you not to try, and how do you know when you need to be stubborn, give it all you've got, and push through? You should know that one of my biggest weaknesses (and strengths) is that as soon as someone tells me I can't do something, I automatically want to do it even more. Naysayers are like fuel for me. When they say no, I feel myself preparing to try again—and try harder and do better.

So what do you do when you suspect someone is telling you no for your own or someone else's good? Do you listen to them, or do you keep trying?

This is important, and I don't think there's an easy answer. But here are four things I like to do when someone is telling me I can't do something.

First of all, give yourself some time to think rationally before you make your decision. I've had to learn it can be really helpful to step back from this crazy thing you're about to try, and wait. And as time passes, every so often I'll get this strange feeling in my gut, this kind of backing down, and I know when that happens, they were right—I can't do it. I need to try something different or come at it from a different angle. Or maybe I can do it, but it would be unwise.

But usually what happens after someone tells me I can't do it is I try to let a few days pass, and if it's not an issue of the safety of myself or others, my desire to do that thing gets even stronger. That's how I know I'm going to keep trying—I *need* to keep trying. And I feel like now I'm going to succeed at it *because* they told me I couldn't. When that thing isn't so much about safety as about expectations or unspoken "rules" or about what others think, it turns into an undying passion for me. And if it's still eating away at you a few days later, or a week later, or a month later, then you know: you have to do it.

You have to try.

You have to keep going.

If you have this undying fire inside you, and you've considered the reasonable concerns, then do it! Don't listen to the people discouraging you. Don't listen to the people who think you can't. Especially when it comes to your passion, the endeavor you've been dreaming about since you were a kid. Pursue it.

Because the thing is, it's up to you. It's your life. I would rather fail while trying than regret not trying at all.

Pay attention to the people who know you, who get you, and who have your best in mind. The people who were trying to convince me to stop making edited videos didn't really know me—I mean, they knew me from the internet, but we hadn't grown up together. They didn't know my heart or my desires or the kind of person I was. They didn't know my long-term goals or the things that made me tick as a human being.

Why did I listen to them?

Just to fit in. To be safe.

My brother, on the other hand, he gets me. He knows what makes me happy. He's been by my side for a long time; he has seen me fail and succeed. He handed me my very first acting part, and he cheered me on when I got it.

He's the one I should have been listening to.

Remember the people around you who will support you without judging. Be aware of their relationship to you, and always remember the history you have with them. If you don't have a good history with someone, take their advice with a grain of salt.

Take a baby step and see what happens. There's nothing wrong with trying. Too many people are afraid of what's going to happen in the future before they even begin. You can't have an effect or live an effective life this way—you have to be willing to fail, and to try again.

For me, I knew my next step was trying to figure out the specs of the standard Vine video. And then it became about consistent posting. And then it became about how to respond to the haters on Vine. Thinking back, everything happened very naturally, very progressively, and if I'd taken a baby step, I'd have known whether to quit or whether to keep going.

If you're unsure about whether not you can achieve your goal, just take that next baby step.

Finally, don't pay attention to your fear. There are plenty of good reasons to *not* try something. Fear isn't one of them. Or more specifically, fear of failure. Never say no to an opportunity or quit pursuing a dream only because you're afraid. The thing is, we're all afraid.

Fear is one of these things in life that you just have to go straight through. If you try to tiptoe around it, you'll end up so far off track you won't even recognize where you are.

Notice I didn't say, "Don't be afraid." We're all afraid. We all end up in situations where we feel like we're in over our heads or missing some key ingredient for becoming successful. But what we have to do is go straight through it.

Looking back, I'm disappointed I paid attention to all that foolishness of those Viners telling me what I could and could not do. I should have put on the blinders, right? Focus on the work! Keep releasing stuff! I should have listened to all of the advice I'm spelling out in these pages. But I was only nineteen years old, and I didn't want to be a bad guy. I didn't want to break the rules and disappoint people. And I let my fear of those things move me in a different direction.

Here's the twist. Literally a month after I made the decision to stop editing videos, guess what happened? In a matter of weeks, Vine changed the platform entirely so you could upload videos from your camera roll. In other words, you could upload edited videos easily, without doing any of the hard work I had done in the beginning.

Everyone started editing their videos.

Even the people who had told me it was lame, that they weren't "real Vines" and they would never do it.

So.

Take your time.

Pay attention to the people who know you the best.

Take small steps in the direction of your dream.

And for goodness' sake, don't let fear guide you.

This is how I try to navigate the space where other people are telling me it can't be done.

In the end, I wonder if the fact that I attempted what most people said would have been impossible, the simple fact that I kept trying, might ultimately have been the reason Vine changed its entire platform altogether.

You never know how big or what type of impact your resilience and willingness to fail can bring.

So, what things are holding you back? Is there something you would love to do but you think is impossible because of other people's expectations of you? What are the things about you that people see and then say, "You can't do it?"

How are you different—more driven, principled, or curious—than everyone else around you, and are people trying to discourage you because of your differences?

Don't listen to the voices.

Don't be afraid.

You can do it.

CHAPTER 3

Noticing the "No"

We've addressed the importance of believing in yourself.

We've talked about those people who tell you that you can't.

But there's an even stranger group of people who end up being obstacles, and these are the people who won't tell you no straight up but will still find ways to hold you back, trying to redirect your energy or keep you doing the status quo.

If you're going to get anywhere, you have to learn to recognize these people and how they influence you. You have to learn to notice the "no," even when it's not obvious. And then you have to figure out how to get past it.

The Seed of a Dream

Two years ago, I decided to create a musical.

That's right, like the ones you see on Broadway. With songs and dance numbers, sets and props. All of it. I wanted to do it.

But not everyone thought it was a great idea.

And not to throw people under the bus, but many of the people who dismissively questioned the idea of the musical were my closest friends and family. They thought I was crazy. And, you know, fair enough. A musical? Why not stay focused on what was working? Why not keep acting, making videos, developing my YouTube audience? Why not keep making money doing what had proven itself?

Most of them had the same reaction to me telling them my idea.

"A musical. Like . . . on the stage?"

Pause.

"Realllly?"

Yes, really.

I know it seemed like it came out of left field (it kinda did), but as soon as I had the idea, my mind was made up. It all started with this little seed that was planted when I was in sixth grade. And it was a seed that remained dormant inside my soul until it sprang out of me at age twenty-four.

It's funny how those things work.

It was my first year at Bak Middle School of the Arts, and it all took place during a showcase. It was the end-of-semester presentation when each grade showed off something they had been working on. The sixth graders went first, performing short scenes. I did a small monologue from *The Lord of the Rings* as Golem. Then the seventh graders did something a little longer and more in depth.

When the eighth graders finally took the stage and started their performance, we hadn't been told what they were going to do, so I had zero expectations. All of a sudden, music started and people began to talk over it, and soon five different people were singing different melodies all in the same song.

My mind was blown.

It was a *musical*. And I had never seen anything like it

before—besides some Disney movies growing up, of course, but nothing this intricate, and never live.

I remember watching all the movement and listening to the sounds and being completely overwhelmed by how beautiful the music was and how the different melodies all meshed perfectly with the music. I felt like I was the only person in the audience—all of my friends were probably whispering and goofing off and trying to pass the time, but to me, in that moment, there was nothing except the music and the performers. How had someone managed to create something with all of these parts moving together so seamlessly? How was this even possible?

I later found out it was a musical called *Into the Woods*. At the time it wasn't a super famous Disney movie. In that incredible experience, my eyes were opened to a beautiful thing for a few hours, and then it was gone.

I went home, never having caught the name of it, and sort of forgot about it. In those days, you couldn't hop on to YouTube and find whatever it was you wanted to watch and learn more about it. So the musical came and went, a blip in my middle school experience, and, to be honest, I lost touch with it. I didn't have another opportunity to experience a musical like that for a long time, and its memory faded. The only thing that remained embedded in my consciousness was a vague melody—"Into the woods to milk the cow, da da, da da, I don't know how"?

Which, of course, was totally not the right lyrics.

But it was enough to remind me that I loved musicals.

Years passed before I saw the movie adaptation of *Into the Woods*, but when I did, I was immediately reminded of what a surreal experience the musical had been for me, of how much I had loved it. It felt like a time machine, and as

I thought back on the musical, I remembered the melodies again—they had stuck with me all that time.

I remembered what a magical experience it had been.

I wondered if that might be something I could do someday.

Sometimes You Have to Do It Yourself

As I said in the last chapter, my usual reaction to someone telling me something can't be done is to try harder. I want to make things happen. I want to overcome obstacles. And looking back, I know that most of my successes come about when I do things in an unconventional, "Marcus Johns" way. I'm successful when I try things that haven't been done before, or at least not often.

Listen: people want you to take the normal route, or a route that makes sense to them. They want you to pay your dues. They want you to stay within accepted processes, because that's what makes *them* comfortable. Try to do something new, do something in a different way, follow an alternative path?

That makes people really uncomfortable.

And people don't like being uncomfortable.

I had this seed in my mind from the first time I saw *Into the Woods*, but I still didn't plan on writing a musical until the day I was on a plane from Los Angeles to Cleveland. I was bored out of my mind and couldn't fall asleep. It was also an older plane with no in-flight entertainment system and no Wi-Fi. So naturally I went to my phone and started to watch older videos I had taken from years back. While scrolling through to pass the time, I came across a video in my camera roll of me singing an improvised song to myself about how I had just bombed an audition. It was funny watching my old self being upset about it and taking out my frustration via song. I remember thinking to myself, *This would be perfect for a musical or something.*

And that was it. *I should make a musical—based on my own life experiences, big or small.*

After all, they say "write what you know," and I *definitely* knew this story.

So that was it. The smallest little thought. *That would work as a scene in a musical.* And my mind just took off.

By now you know that I love challenges, and it just so happened that when I saw that video in my camera roll, I was also at a point in my life where I was asking myself the question, *What's the biggest problem I could create? What's the biggest challenge I could take on, creatively speaking?*

And when I saw that video, I knew the answer.

Make a musical.

And so *Viral: The Musical* was born.

I started writing songs like crazy and wrote fourteen in two weeks. I did nothing but think about the musical. Stuff from the rest of my life, things I had thought were important, suddenly felt a lot less important, and they fell to the side. Things like social media and making YouTube videos. I still did them, but every spare moment I had was spent working on melodies and lyrics and an outline for the story.

To be honest, I don't think my wife, Kristin, knew what to think about it. Initially she probably thought it was just another one of my off-the-wall schemes that I'd eventually drop. (I do get those from time to time.)

As the musical became more of my life focus, I think Kristin probably wondered why I wasn't spending more time on the things that were working for us, things like YouTube videos and generating brand deals. But I was becoming more and more obsessed by this brand-new thing I was creating—it was so daunting and stimulating.

And challenging.

Almost impossible.

I have ADHD (what, you figured that out already?), and some people might use that as another reason to tell me, "Marcus, you can't do this. You can't write a musical. You can't possibly focus the way you need to in order to create something that complex."

But the thing is, my ADHD was actually an advantage. I could go from here to there, from this thing to that thing, and it didn't matter because there was so much to be done. Tired of working on lyrics? Write some music! Bored with melodies? Work on the script! Ready to quit? Draw some stage designs!

Making the musical was a perfect outlet for me, because I have so many interests. As I like to say, I am the *best* at being *mediocre* at everything. Making a musical by myself was perfect, because I needed to do a little bit of everything and have passion for it. And while I may not have been the best at every facet of the process, I definitely had the passion for it.

I wrote more songs. Lyrics. More melodies. Scenes formed in my mind. Character arcs developed. I could start to envision what the set would look like, the backdrops, the props, the costumes.

I was deep into the creation of this musical, yet no one really understood the full picture of what I saw so clearly in my head. If only they could catch the vision, they would trust that it was going to be a hit. But when I talked about it, unsurprisingly, no one took me seriously. Not my friends, family, agency, or managers. They would say things like, "It sounds great; maybe we can get someone to collaborate and develop the idea more." It was a roundabout way of saying no without having to say it. Maybe they thought that if they waited me out, if they sort of let me sit on the idea for long enough, I'd give up and go on to something new. Fair enough. Or I'd go back to the stuff that had worked for me in the past. I can't fault them for thinking that—they weren't in my brain. They couldn't see how much I loved what I was working on, or how determined I was to see it through to a finished product.

Finally, I did a formal pitch to my agency. I lugged my huge keyboard into their offices and played live the entire soundtrack, and I could see the surprise on their faces. It became real to them. And they loved the music and were excited and they finally got on board with the idea.

"So, what's the next step in getting this musical made?" I asked, eager to keep the momentum going.

"Well, we love the songs. But maybe you should bring in another writer to help with the production, the script, that sort of thing. They could help incubate the idea to the next level."

That's when I first started noticing the "no."

I should tell you at this point that I may not be a conventional client. To be completely honest, I may be a little intimidating to work with. I'm outspoken about what I think I should do, and usually I want to do 99 percent of it myself. I don't often listen to conventional wisdom. And in this situation, an agent's job is to package the thing and then bring in other people to make sure it's successful, and what are they supposed to do when their client wants to do it all himself?

They want to take their time, feel their way into it, make

sure there's demand for the product and that the investment will be successful.

Meanwhile, I wanted to get started yesterday, go with my gut, and create something all on my own that will blow people away.

But I agreed. And I waited to work on writing the script myself because they were setting up meetings with writers and producers. But from November to December and into January, I noticed the "no." And look, again, I can't blame them—my vision for the thing was huge. Whenever I asked them where we were, whether or not they had made any good contacts for the musical, I was stonewalled—in a "we're totally on it and not stonewalling you" type of way.

Meanwhile, I kept perfecting it, building out demos, thinking through the script, and soaking in the story. Finally, by the time February rolled around, I couldn't waste another day. I was only getting more and more excited about the idea, and I wasn't getting anywhere this way. So I called my agency.

"Don't worry about finding someone to help me with the musical," I said. "I'm going to write it myself."

"Wait. What, Marcus?"

"The show is based off of my life, so who really knows my story better than me? I'm going to write it myself."

And to that they had no rebuttal.

So I wrote.

For the next four or five months, I wrote the script. Composed the score. Came up with the lyrics. Everything. I realized that no one was going to do this thing for me.

I single-handedly wrote a musical.

Soon after I completed it, I signed with a new agency, and I arrived at one of my first meetings with them to tell them I had written a musical and wanted to get it out there. Up until that point in my life, I had always bowed down to my agents—they do important work, and when you're new to the industry, you can leave everything up to them. But I was no longer sure if that was the best way for me to do things.

"Right now," I said, "this musical is my full-time passion. It's the only thing I'm working on. Either you guys can do this with me or I'll do it on my own. I've already come this far. I can keep going."

Their reaction surprised me. Unlike the veiled noes I had been receiving before, they were surprised, even taken aback, and seemed genuinely excited. I had absolutely no history or success in the musical world, and I'm sure they wondered whether I could pull it off. But if they did, they wisely didn't show it. They were probably also wondering where this kid got that kind of moxie.

After that meeting, I had some hope. They sent it over to a guy who knows Broadway, and he loved it.

"How 'bout you film a table read?" he suggested. "That way we can send it over to one of the musical industry guys and he can listen to the songs, see it all in context."

I loved the idea. But do you know how much work it is to set up a table read? A lot. I had to get all of the music transcribed and formatted in script form. Then I had to print forty copies of the 180-page script and bring a bunch of highly qualified people into my house to read a different part each for a film crew I had to hire. And a sound guy I had to hire. And after all that, it took us an entire day, from early in the morning until late at night, to get it.

But we recorded the table read.

And we sent it to "the guy they knew."

He got back to us the next day.

"Okay, first of all," he began, "I loved it."

He loved it!

"It's great," he continued. "It's actually a show."

It's actually a show!

"Unfortunately, right now, with our contacts, there are only a few people in this space, and none of them are looking for new material."

Wait. What? Talk about the wind rushing out of my sails. That was a big fat "No." Not a "let's talk more about it," or a "I think we might be able to make it work."

Just, "No."

What was I going to do?

Scouting Report: "Lacks a Really Strong Arm"

Prior to the 2000 NFL draft, one of my favorite football players received the following scouting report by a team clearly not interested in having him join their team:

> **Negatives:** Poor build. Very skinny and narrow. Looks a little frail and lacks great physical stature and strength. Lacks mobility and ability to avoid the rush. Lacks a really strong arm. Can't drive the ball down the field and does not throw a really tight spiral. System-type player who can get exposed if he must ad-lib and do things on his own.[2]

How would you respond if this was a scouting report about you? What if someone reviewed your writing or your movie or your photography or your musical with this much criticism?

She's not a good storyteller.

Cinematography isn't his strong suit.

She doesn't have a good grasp of the camera.

He's tentative in delivering his lines.

Would you quit? Become discouraged? Or would you keep going?

Fortunately, the subject of this scouting report didn't quit. This player, the one who "looks a little frail" and "does not throw a really tight spiral," would become one of the greatest quarterbacks of all time—Tom Brady.

He's won three NFL MVP awards, four Super Bowl MVP awards, and a record six Super Bowls.[3] When he retires, he'll go into the Hall of Fame and be remembered as probably the greatest quarterback of all time.

Looks a little frail and lacks great physical stature and strength.

The craziest part is that he had people telling him no long before he reached the NFL draft. During his first year at the University of Michigan, he was the fourth-ranked quarterback on the team. He never even made it out onto the field. His sophomore year was more of the same—practicing, working hard, learning the ropes, competing for a spot on the team . . . and not making it. He made it to third on the depth chart, but he threw only five passes that year.

Anyone else who was told no that many times probably would have quit or transferred to another school, and Brady did think about taking his talents to the University of California, Berkeley. After all, it was closer to home, and he might have a chance to be the starting quarterback. Instead, he decided to stay at Michigan and continue to fight for the starting quarterback position. He was determined to prove everyone wrong.

In his third year, he took over the backup spot, behind Brian Griese. And, finally, in his fourth year at Michigan, he started.[4]

I mean, how many times can one guy hear the word *no* and still keep trying? He never had the strongest arm. He was never viewed as the one with the most talent. But what set him apart was his refusal to quit.

When people said no in subtle and obvious ways, when people told him he couldn't do it, when coaches told him he wasn't good enough, he . . .

Just.

Kept.

Trying.

He recognized the "no," and he let it fuel his determination. He realized that a lot of the people around him didn't think he had what it took. And he kept going.

And he was drafted into the NFL, where nothing changed. Even there, people kept telling him no. And he kept fighting.

There Are No Walls

This is what I've come to realize.

Outside the gates, there are no walls.

Maybe that doesn't make sense yet, so let me explain it. In everything you try to do, there will be gatekeepers standing there, judging you, and then making a pronouncement about whether or not you can go through the gate. Maybe you want to make a movie, and there are the traditional gatekeepers, giving you the yes or no. Maybe you want to write a book—there you've got the agents and publishing houses guarding the gates. Maybe you want to record music, and the record labels are the ones accepting or rejecting you.

They are the gatekeepers. They are guarding the gates.

The crazy thing is, the gates they're guarding don't have walls they're connected to anymore. They're just gates standing there in the middle of wide-open spaces, and anyone can get in now. You can walk right past the gate and get to where you want to be, regardless of whether or not the gatekeepers let you through.

How amazing is that? That's the new world we live in.

Now, will you have to work harder when you go around the gates? Probably. Will you have to do much or all of the work yourself? In most cases, yes. Will you have to spend a little (or a lot) of your own money to make this new thing go without the financial backing of the gatekeepers? Sure.

But listen. There are no walls. You don't have to go through the gates.

There are a thousand different ways to get to your goal, so you can stop listening to the gatekeepers when they tell you you can't do it unless they approve.

When I Went around the Gate (Instead of through It)

"Unfortunately, right now, there are only a few people in this space, and none of them are looking for that type of material."

When we got that news from the influential musical person, I thought to myself, *Really? You exhausted every option and asked everyone in one day?*

Well, maybe that's just how it goes.

I do have to give credit to my agency though. They didn't want to give up.

"We have a few other options," they told me in a very logical voice. "There is still the possibility of doing it in a film or TV version."

I was bummed, but I figured I'd at least hear them out.

"If we do that, what's our next step?" I asked, feeling frustrated.

"We need to attach the idea to the right director."

Again, I realize they were just going about it in the way most people did. They knew the gates that existed, and they knew the gatekeepers, and they knew that if we were going to get this thing made into a TV series or a movie, we needed a big-name director.

But I hadn't spent a year of my life on this project so that I could just hand it over to someone else for them to see it succeed on a platform I didn't originally intend it for. And the idea of it being substantially changed from my initial vision was a depressing thought.

"You know what?" I said. "I'm going to direct it. And it's going to be a musical for the stage, not a movie or a television series."

So they suggested that if I insisted on directing, I should shoot a proof of concept scene from the musical to show my directing chops to producers/production companies. And even though this would be an easy task for me, I was still a bit annoyed at yet another hoop I'd have to jump through to play ball in this industry.

So, I reluctantly agreed to shoot the proof of concept scene while they tried to find me a production company, but I think we all knew it wasn't going to happen. No production company was going to pick this thing up, with me—a complete no-name—as the director and writer. I was just some "social media star," who, by the way, had been on a yearlong hiatus from creating content.

So the months went by with nothing happening. But I had been down this road before, and I was able to recognize this "no" much easier than before.

So, finally, I gave my agency an out.

"If you guys can't move this thing by March 1, then obviously no one is interested," I said. "If we don't have any luck by then, I'll executive-produce it on my own. And I'll foot the bill to produce a local run."

March 1 came, and no one was surprised. People were telling me no without actually telling me no. I recognized that.

"Thanks for all your hard work," I told my agency, and I meant it. They had exhausted all the relevant avenues for me, all the ones they knew to explore, and I understood why it wasn't working out.

So then.

"I'm going to do this thing myself."

And in some ways, that moment was a relief, because, finally, it no longer depended on anyone else. No one else was going to hustle the way I was going to hustle. Care the way I cared. It was all down to me, which was the best *and* the worst part.

In many ways, the story of the musical foreshadowed and mirrored my life during the process of making the musical. For example, in one key scene in the musical, a scene I love so much, the main character Kyle is talking to his agents, and they tell him it's been such a great year in the digital influencer space for him. All Kyle needs to do is keep doing what he's doing, and they'll all be set.

"Actually," Kyle says, "I'd like to do endeavors outside of

social media," and he goes on to explain how he wants to "act or sing and create other forms of art."

The fictional agents double down and claim that it would be ridiculous to leave the very thing that's working. They sing a song called "A Man Is as Good as His Brand" basically saying there's no way he can do it, no way he can break out of this box, and he needs to stick to the plan.

That's life! That's what they're trying to convince him of. This is the way things are. You have to do what you've been given to do.

Everyone's given their box. And that's where you belong. That's who you are.

And look, some of the people who tell you no are simply doing their jobs. This is important to remember. When your parents tell you no, they're fulfilling their parenting duty to protect you as much as possible. When your agent tells you no, they're doing their job—giving you solid, practical advice on how to make money based on proven paths. When a friend tells you no, they're just trying to keep you from getting hurt.

Don't be offended when people tell you no.

But if you have that undying fire to continue, you can't stop. You can hear the "no," and you can consider it, and you can even contemplate quitting, but at the end of the day, you have to decide it's only up to you whether or not you'll do it. And again, if you've considered it and you still feel strongly, you have to keep going.

What to Do When You Recognize the "No"

Maybe you started chasing down your dream. You started putting things in place, doing some hard work, looking around for people to help you along the way. But you keep feeling the "no." It's not that people are outright telling you it can't be done . . . but you can tell by their reactions that they're not completely on board with what you're trying to do, and their unspoken resistance is slowing you down, stealing your momentum, and even potentially killing the project. Here are a few things you can do when you recognize the "no":

First, remain calm. Trust me, I know that feeling of frustration, and when you hit one "no" after another, there will be times when you want to fly off the handle. Were there moments when I wanted to yell at people, shake my head in disgust, or just walk away? Sure. Sometimes I didn't understand. Why weren't the people I trusted helping me get to where I wanted to go? Couldn't they see the vision I was seeing?

I had written something worthwhile, and no one could see it!

But the relationships you have with the people around you are valuable, and it doesn't make sense to destroy friendships or working partnerships just because you're not on the same page or have gotten heated in the moment. This is why I didn't blow off my agent or get sarcastic, like, *Realllly dude, you asked everyone on Broadway if they were interested in one day? Cool, bro.*

There was no point. (Besides, I could just say that in a book later on, and it would feel *so much better!*)

I'm joking. Forgive me.

(But it's true. I have the POWER! I can write whatever I want! HAHAHA.)

Sorry, ADHD.

The point is, totally losing my cool wouldn't serve me

well in the long term. So the first thing to do when you sense the unspoken "no" is to remain calm. No shouting. Don't break anything. Take a deep breath. Know that there is a greater plan and things are going to work out as they're supposed to. Had I not gotten that "no," I wouldn't have had the amazing life experience of producing the show myself!

Don't take it personally. It's so easy, when you first recognize the subtle "no," to feel like people are judging your talent or your ability or your worth as a human being. As creative people, we can get our identities all tied up in the stuff we make, and when people aren't gushing about it, it can feel like someone's looking at your newborn baby and saying, "Yeah, I mean, he's kinda cute. A little bit. Maybe."

The fact is, when you get a "no" from professionals, 99 percent of the time, it's not personal. It's not about you. It's about how the person sees your project and its ability to move through the traditional gateways. (They usually don't know about the whole "there are no walls" thing.) So, don't fault these people—the main problem is that they're still committed to the gatekeeper model. It's all everyone has known for a really long time! Most people remain in that rut (or groove, I guess, depending on how you look at it) for most of their lives, always looking for the endorsements of the people who control the gates. They're not hopeful or thinking creatively enough to see outside the box or find an alternative path.

So when you run into people who doubt that your dream has what it takes to clear the traditional hurdles, don't get upset. Stay calm. Try to see things from their perspective. Try to understand what it is about your dream that's making them hesitate.

It's not about you.

After you remain calm, after you remind yourself not to take it personally, then it's time to . . .

Evaluate your options. The truth of the matter is that creative people have more options these days than ever before when it comes to getting their stuff in front of people. Fifteen years ago, if you had a video you wanted people to see, I guess you could have recorded it somehow, made physical copies, and distributed it to your friends and family. But today you can make the same video in a few minutes, post it to YouTube, and have potentially millions of people view it.

Bam. Just like that.

It's totally unbelievable and insane, isn't it?

The same is true with recording music or self-publishing books. Of course, there are advantages to using a record label or a publishing house, but the point is, they're not specifically *necessary.* If you want to create, if you want people to see your content, you can walk around those gates now, because the walls have been removed because of the internet. Information is free, and communication is instant and universal!

So when you start to see the "no," take stock of where you're at. Evaluate your options. Talk to others who make the same stuff you're making.

Gain some perspective and consider the true situation. Is it something you *can* possibly do if you apply some effort and enlist the help of some friends? In my experience so far, this kind of creative thinking has served me well. Give it a try, and I believe you'll find your way.

Keep going. This may be the last one on the list, but it's actually one you need to keep in mind at all times—from the very first time you sense the unspoken "no" to the point you're tempted to take the rejection personally, and all the way through to when you have to begin listing your options. You have to keep going. You can't give up.

There were plenty of times during the creation of this musical, and all the endless meetings and dead ends and questions, when I thought it might be a good time to give up. Walk away from it. I knew I could keep making a living doing what I had been doing before, and everyone was telling me that's what I should be doing.

But that wasn't good enough. I had a drive to see this thing exist, so I didn't give up.

And eventually it paid off, and now I know it will continue to!

The View from the Scaffolding

Fast-forward to the opening night of the musical. I sat on the scaffolding with my two co-stars in the show and waited for the curtain to open for that first time. They were so chatty, but I was trying to focus on my lines, on the music. Then the overture began. I could hear the music swelling—this music I had written that took me the past two years to develop. Finally being played by a live orchestra. Behind the music, I could hear the audience too, rustling and finding their seats.

Even after all the months of work and years of waiting, the whole night sort of snuck up on me in a way I hadn't expected. For days, probably weeks, I had built it up so much in my head as the process progressed. What would opening night be like? How would I feel? Would I get emotional? I had no idea! But in my mind, it was this monumental thing that would change my life.

But it wasn't like that at all.

In fact, it reminded me of getting married to Kristin. Before the wedding day, you think getting married is going to change everything. And I guess in some ways it does, but my relationship with Kristin didn't magically change on that day. One moment we were engaged, and the next we were walking down the aisle, married. But I was still Marcus and she was still Kristin. We were both the same people. Sure, we had rings on our fingers, and we had made a vow. It was still us, but it was the "us" we had become over time. It was the work we put in over time that made our relationship. It was the years of long distance and the struggles that formed us into a strong love. The wedding day didn't make us into that; it was just the confirmation of that fact.

It was a different kind of magic than I expected.

The same was true of the play. We were preparing that space for what felt like an eternity, loading equipment, assembling the set, and getting the sound and lights configured. We were running lines and practicing the dance breaks. Memorizing our harmonies. Those days took on a routine kind of feel, so that by the time the show started, it felt like the next logical thing. It wasn't as momentous as I had imagined it would be. But it was the years of work and struggle and overcoming the noes that ended up being the rewarding part.

I leaned over to the two other characters in that opening scene, and we said a little prayer. And of course, there was that crazy special moment when the curtain opened and the audience roared, then quieted, and I said my opening line.

I had done it. We had done it.

You can do it too. But prepare yourself to recognize the

unspoken no, and when it comes up, because it will, remember to stay calm, get some perspective, and listen to your own inner voice telling you what to do.

There's a different kind of magic than you may expect.

In learning to read, I owe almost as much to the bitter opposition of my master as to the kindly aid of my mistress. I acknowledge the benefit of both.

FREDERICK DOUGLASS

CHAPTER 4

Overcoming Stereotypes

Success is one of the things that pretty much all of us in the world think we want.

We want to do our work well, and we want to be recognized for it.

You want to know one of the main problems with success?

Wait, you may be thinking. *There's a problem with success?*

There is. Actually, there are lots of them, but here's one of the biggies: once you prove you can do it, once you show people you know how to do something well, everyone expects you to forever and always stay in that lane.

It's true.

If you write an award-winning mystery novel, they expect you to keep writing mysteries. If you write acclaimed rap music, in their mind you're a rapper. If you make your name photographing cute little baby hippopotamuses, well, you get the point. They will always expect you to keep doing more of the same.

Always.

Even harder, they'll start to create in their minds a whole new list of things you can't do—basically, anything besides the thing you already did well. Because someone who is really, really good at something can't possibly be any good at something else.

That's what they think.

When it comes to people who know me in the industry, I'm the digital guy. I'm the social media guy, the YouTuber, the ex-Viner, and the videomaker who can draw a crowd online. Marcus is the wacky, zany, crazy guy who will jump off buildings or shout random stuff and make people laugh. In interviews, I could tell people thought I was just a goofy dummy, and they'd want me to say something zany off-the-cuff, right on the spot. They thought there wasn't anything more to me than that guy in the videos, and the reporters were always waiting in expectation for me to do something bizarre.

I'm telling you, once you reach a certain level of success, it's hard to break out of the groove people put you in, especially when they think that thing is all you can do.

You know what makes it even harder to break out of the mold?

When *you* think that's all you can do. When *you* believe the voices claiming you're one-dimensional, a flat character, someone who is completely predictable.

I know, because for a long time I believed the stereotype that people had of me. I figured the best thing to do was to keep focusing on what had worked for me in the past. I should keep being funny, keep making videos, keep engaging on social media.

But I had other dreams too, dreams I wanted to believe.

I wanted to believe I could be a director. I wanted to believe I could write a musical. I wanted to believe I could sing and do some of these other things. But I had never done anything to prove that I could, even to myself.

Have you had success in one area and then people tried to pigeonhole you into that forever?

Most people have. So how do you break out from and overcome those stereotypes?

Gaining Confidence

When I was a Viner, I had this strong idea for a new kind of television experience. I know, I know—of course I'm going to say it was a strong idea, because it was my idea! But I'm telling you, it was seriously good and had all kinds of potential. I'm not even going to say what the idea was because I still believe in it and I don't want anyone to steal it until I can try it!

We pitched it to different people, and there was a lot of interest. As soon as we told people what we wanted to try to do, they started nodding their heads and I could see it in their eyes—they were interested. They thought it was a good idea. They wanted to do it.

But everyone, after a few days of thinking about it, returned to me with the same feedback.

"We love the idea. We'd like to do it, and of course you can be in it because it was your idea, but we'll get someone else to direct it and produce it. You're a social media guy. We need someone with experience. We need a big name."

They had a stereotype of who I was and what I could do, and it didn't include directing and producing.

Ouch.

That hurt.

Then I did the musical, and I proved to everyone (including myself) that I could write and direct and compose and do all of these different things in places where people hadn't taken me seriously. I had been a Viner for a long time, and I was confident in that space, which is cool—it's great to have an area you know you're strong in. But I'm the kind of person who, once I achieve one thing, wants to try something else. I wanted something different, and making the musical gave that to me. Actually, it didn't only give me that feeling of trying something new; it made me even more certain I wasn't the kind of person who would do one thing for my entire life. I wanted, even more, to move into new areas, new experiences.

Ever since creating and putting on the musical, I feel like I can do anything. I know I can. Because when you do something outside the box of what people expect you to do, or when you successfully accomplish something daunting that felt like a huge challenge? It gives you a boost of confidence in every area of your life.

Ever since I did the musical, I'm a braver person. I'm even more creative and less apt to listen to the naysayers.

But you should have known me in high school.

When I was sixteen years old and a sophomore, well before Vine, I was in my second year of student government, and people knew me as the wacky student body rep (no idea where they got that impression). I hosted the pep rallies and tried to bring some fun into student government (talk about taking on a challenge!). But if you would have asked anyone else in that group, they would have told you I had a very limited role. I wasn't seen as an organizer or an innovator by any means. When they needed someone to bring up the energy level, I was their guy, but they purposely avoided giving me any major responsibilities because, well, I don't know, I guess because I was Marcus.

I was the goofy dude.

I was the one who made people laugh.

I was *not* the organized one who got things done.

But that year, when I was in tenth grade, I felt an urge to do something different. I can't remember why. I liked building stuff, I liked being hands-on with visual arts, and I started to ask myself a question—one that seems to echo at different points in my life.

What's the biggest challenge I could take on in my life right now?

It's the same question I asked that led me to my first audition and had me putting videos on Vine and even making the musical. I've been asking myself this question for a long time, and it's led to my best adventures, my biggest failures, and my most unpredictable successes.

And each time, I've sincerely wanted to know: *What's the biggest challenge I could take on?*

When I was a sophomore in high school, the answer to that question seemed like "organizing the homecoming dance." That was the biggest event in my world at the time. Do you remember something that was a big deal when you were sixteen years old? I decided that's what I was going to do—I was going to take on the responsibility of organizing and putting on the homecoming dance, and for some reason the rest of the team decided to let me do it.

I kind of have to wonder what they were thinking.

There were plenty of voices that immediately questioned the decision.

"Zany Marcus is going to be in charge of homecoming?"

"Can he actually do anything besides make people laugh?"

"This is going to be a disaster."

"He can't do it!"

Well, there I was, organizer of the homecoming dance. What was I going to do? I created a team of people willing to help out with some of the various responsibilities, and we got to work.

One of the toughest parts of the whole experience was when I realized that there were even some people on my own team who didn't believe in me, who doubted that I could lead the effort. Working with them got more and more difficult, more and more frustrating, because their doubt started coming through more. I soon realized I could give them simple things to do, straightforward tasks, but it'd work best if it wasn't things that had to do with carrying out the bigger parts of my vision. It got to be too much work to try to answer all the questions—questions that mostly served to poke holes in the plan and undermine the ideas, from the decor, to the setup, even the way to go about doing basic things. So rather than argue with them, I determined to prove them wrong.

I stopped working closely with the doubters and focused my energy on the students who believed we could do it, and do it well. They were the ones I bounced ideas off, the ones I relied on to be creative and do the things that would require some real energy to complete.

We had a long hallway in our high school that led to the gym, and one of our primary responsibilities for the homecoming dance was to deck it out from top to bottom. It was one of the best parts to have that hallway look amazing when everyone arrived. I'd decided on a Las Vegas theme, and the team and I went all out.

And as we worked to prepare for that big event, at some point I realized, *Hey, this is working. People are into it, and they're making it happen with me. Maybe I do have great ideas for something like this, and maybe my energy and unique talents are useful and not just entertaining. And when I put my mind to it, maybe I do have the discipline to make it happen.*

In my mind, the whole thing just kept taking on a bigger scope, so I proposed that we decorate inside the gym too, where the dance was held. Surprisingly, it had never been done before—usually they just put up a banner in the gym, but I wanted to keep going. Maybe we could hang stuff from the ceiling and bring in more lights and create a stage set.

And again, I got hit with the "no."

"Kid, you can't do that. You can't hang lights in here. You can't hang stuff from the gym lights. They'll never let you do that."

You can't do it!

Once again, it's probably best to assume you'll hear this a lot if you decide to try to break out of the stereotypes people have chained you to.

Maybe I could, and maybe I couldn't. And to be fair, I didn't even know if the hallway was going to fully come together yet. But I knew one thing: I was determined to make this the best homecoming dance our school had ever seen. And I didn't care if people thought I was incapable or unorganized or too young or whatever.

But would that new confidence be enough?

Reinvention

I absolutely love people who reinvent themselves. I love it when actors become directors, when athletes from one sport move into a different sport, or when musicians change genres. It takes a lot of guts to make those kind of switches, especially when they've already been massively successful at what they originally did. And it takes a particular kind of brave willingness to get out of your comfort zone.

One of the first people who comes to my mind when I think of breaking out of stereotypes started his career as a guy doing sketch comedy on Fox. From there he went on to leading roles in some major comedy films, quickly establishing himself as "a bankable comedy actor."[5]

Maybe you know who I'm talking about—clearly I'm a big fan of his: Jim Carrey.

During his heyday, he had three major movies release . . . in the same year! *Ace Ventura: Pet Detective*, *The Mask*, and *Dumb and Dumber* all released in 1994, and Carrey immediately became a household name. By 1996, he had signed with Sony to star in *The Cable Guy* for $20 million. He had landed lead role after lead role, and his brand of physical, zany comedy was clearly connecting with people.

And that's when he started to reconsider the direction his career was taking.

Crazy, right?

He was getting $20 million per movie, and he wasn't satisfied. He wanted to make a change.

The thing is, he didn't want to be known as only a funny actor—he wanted to take on more serious roles and prove that he could act in anything, play any character. But who would cast him in anything other than a comedy? Could someone who made their name on laugh-out-loud scenes do something more dramatic? His face and crazy body movements had become a brand, and it was hard for those around him to imagine him doing anything else.

Wouldn't it be better to just keep doing what he was doing, keep making money, keep being funny?

That wasn't good enough for him.

So even after *The Cable Guy* wound up being disappointing to most people, he decided to go completely out of the box and try out for a role that would shatter the stereotypes people had of him.

He auditioned for the lead role in *The Truman Show*, and he landed the part.

"It's not Shakespeare," he said in a 1998 interview with *Entertainment*, "but it's a more human character than any I've done. It's a movie about life, unrequited love, the need to accomplish something you've never been able to. It's like a Chaplin thing, with funny characters and whimsy and laughs. But it's got serious undertones and issues."[6]

And it worked. The movie was a huge success and even garnered some Academy Award talk. The risk had paid off, and Carrey moved into an entirely new space of acting during the next decade. He established himself as a multidimensional actor, going on to star in movies like *Eternal Sunshine of the Spotless Mind*, even occasionally returning to his roots in comedy.

Do you want to break out of the stereotypes people have of you?

Jim Carrey was prepared to risk his career and livelihood on a move into a completely different area of acting.

How much are you prepared to risk?

Ways to Break the Stereotype

Of course, not everyone who tries to break the stereotype is successful. Michael Jordan stopped playing basketball to try his swing in minor league baseball for two seasons. His foray, while not a complete failure, definitely didn't propel him into baseball's major leagues, and he would eventually return to basketball. His reputation in the NBA remained strong (he won three more championships), but his time in baseball is seen more as a blip than a success.

So how do you know if people are right? Should we escape the stereotypes that people have formed about us, or should we stay in our lane? Hopefully you've guessed by now what I think.

Be willing to take a risk. Stereotypes exist for a reason. A lot of the time, they fit. And I think a lot of people wish they could break out of the stereotypes, but often there's a lot at stake, and that can make anyone hesitate.

Sometimes you risk losing income. Other times you risk losing your reputation. People remember the great things you already did, so what if you're not as successful? What if you take the risk, break out of your stereotype, and then it all flops? Not only does this new failure hurt, but you might not be able to go back to your original work, or people might not have the same respect for you afterward. And even if this new thing ends up being a huge success, in the time it took to change direction, you took time away from the thing that originally made you great in the first place—a move that probably cost you money.

So, you have to be willing to take a risk. You have to look at all the things you stand to lose and then still move forward. This kind of decision isn't an easy one to make.

When I changed direction and focused on the musical, I risked losing money, losing the interest of my online following, and losing the potential followers who would have come on board during that downtime. I also risked losing brand deals, since I wasn't making as many videos anymore. There was a lot on the line, and no guarantees that if I came back to the online world after making the musical, anyone would be waiting for me in that space.

I had to decide whether or not it was worth the risk.

Now that it's behind me, in hindsight, was it?

Totally.

But you have to ask yourself: *Am I prepared to take a risk?*

Prove to people you're willing to work hard. Until people see you doing this new thing firsthand, they're going to doubt you, and you really shouldn't be hard on them for this. It's only natural. People expect us to keep doing what we're doing.

One of the ways you can move them away from their doubt is by working harder than anyone else. People appreciate that, and even if the end result is a little off, they see how determined you are to improve, and they will often give you a little bit of grace for that.

Would I have continued to pursue the musical if I had known from the beginning that I was staring down a two-year journey filled with twists and turns and rejection and a serious amount of financial investment? I don't know. That's a great question. Maybe I wouldn't have done it. But now people have seen how hard I'm willing to work, and they're seeing the result of all that work in the musical I created, and they're sitting back, somewhat surprised. I've proven myself to be more, and they see me in a new way. I can feel it—this confidence that people have in me—because they saw the work I put in.

If you're willing to take this huge risk, to break out of the stereotypes that people have of you, then make sure you're prepared to work harder than you ever have before. Hard work will make up for a lot of mistakes you might make.

Find, and work with, people who believe in you. Not everyone is going to believe in you. Like most of those in student government when I planned the homecoming dance, people around you will sometimes only be able to see who you've been and what you've done up to that point. There will be a lot of people who hesitate to go with you toward this new goal.

But there will always be at least an enthusiastic few who can see the vision. They'll be eager to support you. These are the people you have to focus your time and energy on. Don't worry about trying to convert the doubters! Rally the ones who believe in the new vision; honor and utilize them in ways that are exciting and important, and you'll have a much better chance of hitting your goals and overcoming the stereotypes.

Be confident. The worst thing you can do is make a major change, one that shatters the stereotypes people have of you, and do it half-heartedly.

I'm serious. That's the worst thing you can do.

You absolutely have to believe in yourself and be willing to go all in. If you don't, you'll just sabotage yourself from the very beginning and it will all go up in flames, and then you'll still be left wondering if it would have worked out if you would have given it 100 percent. In other words, you'll have the losses of the risk without any of the lessons or knowledge you could have gained.

Can you imagine if I would have volunteered to do the homecoming dance but later in the same meeting expressed how afraid I was that I didn't have what it would take?

Can you imagine if I would have done all that work for the musical and then on opening night stood in front of the cast, orchestra, and stage crew and portrayed an image of doubt and uncertainty?

Once you make the call, once you decide to start this new thing, believe in yourself. This goes all the way back to chapter 1. Do what you have to do to get rid of those negative voices in your head, the ones telling you that you can't do it, and plow ahead.

Finally, speak your new dream out loud. This is how every seed of an idea starts to germinate: you have to *say it out loud*. Most people don't understand the power of speaking things into life, or even if they do, they're afraid, because one of the hardest parts of breaking the stereotypes is telling your friends and family about this crazy new idea you want to try. You probably know ahead of time what their skepticism will look like and how you'll look in their eyes, but you can't let that worry you. If you're willing to risk and work hard, you have to commit to share this new dream. You have to be all in. You have to describe it and give them the opportunity to come with you or not.

If you don't jump in like this, you'll never get people to follow you. But once you start speaking it to life, articulating what the end is going to look like, you cast the vision. Some of those around you may still drag their feet, but some of them will also come with you. You'll learn a lot through the process, and it may not look the way you originally intended, but saying it out loud will go a long way to making this crazy dream of yours come to life.

I'm still going through all of these things today. The first stereotype I had to break was that of me creating a musical. I've proven I can do it, but now I want to take the musical on tour, and it will cost a lot of money. This is just another version of stereotype breaking, and everyone keeps telling me that's not how musicals are done. That's not how they're performed. That's not how they become successful.

You know what? Maybe they're right!

But I've developed fans all over the country through the viral videos I've made. There are people out there who I believe would come and watch the musical if we brought it to them.

The truth is, I don't know for sure. When you're taking a risk, there's a lot you don't know. That's what makes it a risk. I just keep sitting in these meetings and listening and then saying, "Yeah, we can do it. We can take this thing on the road." And every week, I get new ideas about it. It's exciting to me.

When most people see a roadblock, they think it means they can't go any further. Most people see a roadblock and sit down, or go in the opposite direction and give up on that road. But when I see a roadblock, I can't help but take in the open highway on the other side. Some of the most exciting things that have happened to me in my life were waiting on the other side of the roadblock!

When I see a roadblock, I start looking around.

I kick at it.

I test it.

I'm always thinking, *There has to be another way around this thing.*

Don't let the roadblocks between you and something completely new keep you from moving forward. Be willing to take a risk. Work hard with people who believe in you. Be confident and speak your dream out loud.

You're going to surprise everyone.

Even yourself.

Shocking Everyone

The day of the homecoming dance finally arrived. We had put all of this work into preparing for that one night. We had built props, painted flyers, and had an entire team decorate the hall and the gym, which so many people had said couldn't be done.

And yes, they let us hang lights in the gym. And yes, we did knock down a light, as some naysayers had predicted—and it basically exploded.

But you know what? Not everything will go according to plan.

But that's another story for another day.

We welded a giant Eiffel Tower and created the Paris Las Vegas casino with its huge hot air balloon. We did so many unconventional things, and everything looked awesome. When people came into the dance that night, they were in awe. I watched their expressions as they came down the hall, the surprise on their faces when they entered the gym. We had done it. Everyone was shocked.

I went for it, went big, and it worked out.

Me—the goofy, zany, unpredictable member of student government. Yes, I had organized and decorated one of the best dances in school history, in my humble opinion.

I can tell you this, based not just on the story of the homecoming dance but also on so many other things I've done in my life: when you successfully break out of a stereotype, when you do something amazing that shocks everyone around you, when you prove you're not only that one kind of person they thought you were . . . it feels incredible.

It's so freeing.

It makes you believe that anything is possible. Anything!

It's one of the most thrilling experiences in life.

When I showed up at the student government meeting the following week, people looked at me differently. They talked to me with more respect. They listened when I said things. They took my ideas seriously.

When opening night of the musical was over and the curtain came down, when I celebrated with the rest of the cast and crew, when I mingled with the crowd afterward, I was on cloud nine. I had accomplished something no one thought I could do. And I felt it again, that kind of surprised respect.

You can do it too.

You're not only what everyone knows you for. You're not only the work you've done up until now. There are untapped areas of creativity inside you, things you can do that are completely outside of what you've already done.

This new thing you so badly want to do? The thing that falls completely outside of your realm of expertise and experience?

That's right: *you can do it!*

You're going to fail.

Miserably.

Horribly.

Often.

And probably even on your next endeavor, at least in some way.

But wait, I hear you think to yourself. *I thought this was supposed to be a motivational book*.

You thought I was going to be lifting you up with all kinds of encouragement, playing off of the ironic title (*You Can't Do It!*) so I could actually show you that you can do it?

Well, news flash! . . .

Yeah, you're actually right.

But here's the thing: failure will always be part of your journey.

Always.

However, this shouldn't depress you. Actually, with the right mind-set, the idea of failure will empower you and motivate you to keep going.

Pay attention now.

In the entertainment world, there are countless rejections and failures you have to endure. Audition after audition, pitch after pitch, and even when you get your chance, the reviews of that project you finally landed could be horrible. And there goes your steam. It makes you want to just quit, blame the system, and move on. It's the same in the publishing world, the music industry, the business world, and in almost every creative sphere in life. As a creator or artist, you find it especially difficult, because rejection of your work is so closely tied to your identity. Your art is a direct reflection of you and your creative expression.

But some people make it through. They get the dream roles. Their song charts after years of creating music. Their hundredth business venture finally takes off and becomes a Fortune 500 company. Somehow those people had the fortitude to press through the pain of rejection.

These people understand it best that "being an overnight success takes a lifetime."

However, I've learned that just because successful creative people frequently encountered and overcame their failures doesn't mean the sting of failure is something they no longer feel. Or more specifically, that they enjoy the pain in the moment. They don't. No one likes the feeling of failure. But with repetition they also learn just how temporary the pain of failure is and how long-lasting the effects of knowledge and experience gained from that failure are. They develop the fortitude to stay in the game longer, and because of this, they get their breakthrough.

The thing is, failure doesn't have to have a lasting sting. The fact that failure is always a possibility doesn't have to ruin the experience or take the joy out of this new thing you're trying. All you have to do is get to the point where you can accept the fact that failure will often be part of your journey and start to see what failure truly represents—and yes, even how it helps you.

One acting role I got years ago was that of a Canadian police officer in a show. I was pretty pumped about it because it was a serious drama, something I hadn't been able to do before, something that allowed me to branch out from the usual silly guy comedy routine.

I remember that as we were starting to get into preproduction, the director told me early on that I didn't have to worry about using a Canadian accent.

"Just focus on the character," the director said.

But for some reason, I got it stuck in my head that the character wouldn't be the same without the accent. I remember how I stressed out about trying to have a good Canadian accent (which is really stupid because the accent is so similar to an American accent, and it wasn't necessary for the character). The first day on the set came, and we shot takes for the first episode. I remember asking for more takes for certain scenes because I felt like I wasn't doing a good accent. Once again, the director reassured me it was fine and to totally forget about trying to do an accent. We had to move on. But how could I totally forget it? I was going to have a thick Canadian accent in the first episode and none in the rest? That would look so stupid! I couldn't have that.

For the rest of the time I tried way too hard, trying to match my performance in the first episode, and the accent didn't come off very well. Actually, it was pretty awful.

In fact, there was one episode where my performance (and my accent) were both so bad that I couldn't bear watching it. I hoped, by some miracle, that no one else in the world would watch it. Maybe it would air while some other worldwide disaster was taking place, and no one would tune in for my horrifying performance.

Of course, when Kristin watched it, she was encouraging, but to me it felt like a massive failure.

You know what?

Sometimes you have to accept the times you don't do a good job.

Sometimes you have to learn to acknowledge it and then move on.

Sometimes you just have to shake your head and tell yourself you'll do better next time. It will be fine.

So I had a bad Canadian accent! Sue me!

Yet while that show was a painful experience for my ego, it wasn't my biggest failure.

Not even close.

In Which I Decide to Hop a Train with My Friends and Ride It Cross-Country

Toward the end of my Vine days, I made a video that would eventually lead to one of my bigger projects . . .

Which would lead to one of my biggest failures.

I was doing all kinds of random, crazy things in those Vine days, and I had always wanted to jump on a train. I don't know. It's just this culturally American thing, isn't it? The idea of hopping on a train and just taking it to the end of the line, wherever that is, riding across the country and seeing everything there is to see—the cities, the mountains, the plains, the coast. There's something about hopping trains that goes deep into the American psyche. Just crazy, dangerous freedom.

I remember one day on my way home from Ultimate Frisbee practice (yes, I was on the frisbee team in college), a train was going by. I parked the car and ran over to it and jumped on. I used the footage in a six-second Vine while I shouted, "I've always wanted to do this!" The train wasn't moving that fast, and I hopped right back off again. I laughed, and it could have easily been a one-and-done occurrence.

But the thrill of that short ride stuck with me. Something about it—the slow, determined movement; its mysterious destination; the power it evoked from the clacking sound it made on the tracks—got into my blood.

One of my classmates saw the video of me jumping on the train, and the next time we were in class, he told me he had done it too. That he had hopped on a train years before. But his experience hadn't been as quick and innocent as mine.

"Seriously?" I asked. I thought that anyone who was crazy enough to jump on a train was definitely my kind of person. I wanted to hear more.

"Yeah," he said, but he wasn't laughing. "Someone told me about train hoppers and how you can go all over the country, so I wanted to try it. I figured I'd ride for a couple of miles and then get off. Problem is, I didn't know what I was doing when I jumped on. The train started going faster and faster, and after the first minute it became too fast for me to get off. And I wasn't inside a car or on a flat surface where I could sit or lie down—I was hanging on for dear life to a ladder on the side of an oil tanker for hours going seventy miles an hour. I honestly thought I was going to fall off and die. I didn't know how long I could hang on."

My eyes were wide at this point. What a story! My heart was pounding just thinking about it.

"What did you do?" I asked.

"I just hung on, man. I thought that was it. I locked my

arm in the ladder as best I could and kind of wedged myself in, crying the whole way."

"How'd you get off?" I asked.

"I rattled along from Tallahassee all the way to Jacksonville. I thought I'd be on it for ten minutes, but three hours later, it stopped. I had to have a friend drive all the way out there to pick me up."

My imagination took off.

Maybe you would think that hearing about someone who had a death-defying incident while train hopping would discourage a normal person from trying it. But it's me we're talking about here.

The truth is, the whole time he was telling me this story, one thought was racing through my mind: *I have to do this. I have to jump on a train and ride it across the country.*

What really excites me is doing things where I know I'm in over my head. I don't know why, I love just jumping in, having no idea what I'm doing, and figuring it out from there. When I see something I haven't been trained to do but think I might be good at, I mean even remotely, I can't stop myself from trying it. It was that way with my first audition when I was ten years old. It was that way with Vine, when I felt like I was late to the game but excited to give it a try.

And it was that way with hopping on trains.

I knew nothing about train hopping. Nothing. Well, that's not entirely true—I did know it was illegal. But that sort of added to the mystique of it all. The thought of running along the tracks at night and sneaking onto a train car, maybe waking up and watching the sun rise, seeing the landscape roar by.

There's a natural progression for me when I get new ideas, and it is as follows:

1. Get new idea.
2. Do it right away.

And this pattern didn't change any when it came to train hopping.

Something else I love doing is pulling other people into my schemes, mostly because I love living vicariously through others. Even if I do something a thousand times, I get to relive that first thrill by watching someone else do it for the first time. It's one of my favorite feelings. Sure, I love going outside of my comfort zone, but I love even more getting other people outside of theirs. It's one of the underlying reasons I'm writing this book—to inspire you to get out of your comfort zone and try something new. It really is the best!

Four friends agreed to join me on this adventure, old friends from elementary and middle school. The plan was to hop trains all the way from Los Angeles to New York City and to complete it in under thirty days. I did a ton of research on how to (illegally) board a train, how to find and read train schedules and tell where each train was headed, what the best kind of cars to ride on were, and as much safety stuff as I could find.

I love looking back over that documentary, watching the beginning when I filmed myself having conversations with each of my friends and their different reactions to the idea. A couple of them were excited and said yes immediately. A couple of them were pretty hesitant and took some convincing. But at the end of the day, all five of us set out on this crazy trip.

We spent a couple of nights by the tracks in Los Angeles, watching the trains, trying to figure out which ones would be the best to ride, which ones would put us on the right track. When the night finally came for our departure, we had our backpacks filled with gear and camping supplies and our cameras ready to roll. Our train pulled into the yard as we hid under a bridge. As it slowly crept by, the five of us jogged out into the light and tried to find a good "pig with wings"—that's what they call a flatbed train car carrying a semi-truck with aerodynamic wings on its undercarriage. Those are perfect for riding, because we could climb underneath the semi and have some shelter. They also hide you on the sides from the police officers who roam the tracks looking for people like us who are riding illegally.

Finally, a series of them rolled past, and we ran to the ladder, pulled each other onto the train, and were on our way. It was such a rush! We pulled wet handkerchiefs up over our mouths to filter the thick diesel smog and soot as we rolled through tunnels and out of the city. Underneath us, the ground flew past—sometimes as fast as seventy-five miles per hour.

When the sun rose over the mountains the next morning and the tracks curved away from us in both directions, it was the most amazing feeling ever. We cruised north toward Bakersfield and into the start of an incredible journey.

I'll never forget that trip.

Afterward, I was completely convinced we'd be able to create a documentary and sell it to a multi-channel network (MCN) for good money. In those days, people were snatching up content all over the place, and I thought my documentary would be the kind of thing they'd love.

At that point, my management advised me not to do the editing myself. I had hundreds of hours of footage, and, to be honest, I didn't even know where to begin. They pushed me to hire a documentary editor, so I agreed and went that route. I paid someone $17,000 to edit *Yard Boys* for me, and while I wasn't crazy about doing it, I went along with it because, like I said, I was convinced we would sell the documentary for at least $50,000. I figured it was just the cost of doing business.

But even after I got it back from the editor, it was way too long, so I ended up doing a detailed edit myself. It wasn't that he didn't do a good job; it was just that I had a vision in my head for what I wanted it to be, and the edited version I received just wasn't it.

When I sat down and started to do the work myself, it felt good. It felt right. Once I started grinding away at it, a little every day, I knew I was on the right track.

It's like making a sculpture, right? You just chisel away at it, and the thing is going to be an ugly chunk of rock for a really long time.

This is a huge problem for a lot of us—we try to avoid failure by avoiding the work. We procrastinate, keep putting it off, because we're scared of what might happen or how we might fail or what might go wrong. Sometimes it's a lot easier to hold on to a dream than it is to try to make that dream a reality.

The problem with that mind-set is that you never get past the "ugly chunk of rock" phase. It's engaging in the work that helps you turn it into something beautiful.

That had been me for a little while, avoiding the work, but once I took it on, once I started editing, I enjoyed it.

But the situation got worse. As I finished editing and we started thinking about how to market it to MCNs, I butted heads with a friend of mine who was involved in the project, and he ended up holding it hostage, keeping me from releasing it. This caused major delays. More issues. None of my friends had signed releases because I never asked them to. I thought it seemed unnecessary. They were my friends!

But then all of these things combined to further delay the project.

The MCNs stopped snatching up content.

I wasn't being as active on social media.

I was left holding the $17,000 editing bill and a documentary that no one was interested in buying. It was a rough feeling.

Eventually, I just put it up on YouTube. I didn't make any money from it—in fact, I lost money.

I had no idea what I could do to salvage it.

Blessed with a History of Failure

Turns out failure kind of runs in the family. I mean, we've had successes, but it's watching my parents fail, and seeing their reaction to that failure, that has been so inspiring for me.

Take their "Pump Prop," for example.

I know—what could possibly go wrong with a product named the Pump Prop?

My mom and dad developed the Pump Prop soon after they were married, back in the ancient days when gas pumps didn't have those little metal nozzle clips to keep the gas flowing. There weren't many in use yet, and in some places they weren't allowed. Whatever the case, there was no easy way to keep the gas pump on other than standing there and holding it. I guess some people had tried using their wallets or other objects they found in their car, with mixed results.

My parents' idea for the Pump Prop was basically a piece of plastic shaped like a trapezoid (a lopsided rectangle) that fit perfectly in that space and held the gas pump in the on position. It had little ridges and bumps so it would stay in place. They had even made one side of it an ice scraper for people up north to scrape off their windshields.

Practical, easy to use. They could have sold thousands and made a mint.

They ended up spending a ton of money on it just to get it off the ground. They had to pay for a certain number of the device to be made up front. I don't know the details, but I know it was a substantial amount for my parents at the time—they were newly married. In fact, they spent a good chunk of their savings.

But it didn't work out. They just couldn't sell enough to make the venture work. And, eventually, companies started making/allowing the pumps with the little clips still used today.

We always had a plastic Pump Prop in our cars growing up, and I thought they were just some random old tool my parents liked, but when they told me they had invented it, it blew my mind. It seemed so legit to me because I always saw them around and thought it was a big brand.

"Well, I definitely want one for my car!" I said.

I thought it was cool my dad had invented something. After all, this hadn't been in the *Shark Tank* days, where you had the internet to help you sell stuff, where you could make announcements to all your friends on social media or even on email. Theirs had been a complete grassroots effort. My dad had packaged the Pump Prop himself, pounded the pavement, and tried to get garages and gas stations to carry it in their stores.

"That's amazing, Dad," I said. I was totally impressed by his creativity.

"Yeah." He shrugged. "We got it into a few gas stations, and we sold a couple of them, but we lost money on it. A lot of money."

He didn't seem too bothered by the failure. That interested me. I thought if I had lost a lot of money trying something, I might feel pretty bitter about it. But my dad was definitely not bitter. He later showed me how we still had boxes of Pump Props twenty-plus years later in our attic.

"Do you wish you hadn't done it?" I asked. I wondered if whenever he saw that box, he'd have feelings of regret. It was a pretty major failure, and it happened early in his life too. I'm sure they would have loved to have spent that money on something else.

But Dad just shook his head.

"Not at all," he said. "We thought it was a great idea. There was a huge potential upside. It didn't work out, but that's just life. If I hadn't done it, I'd always wonder. You know?"

I knew exactly what he meant.

I'm sure there was more to the conversation, but what really stuck with me was that my dad didn't have major regrets about losing all that money. I thought that was really cool. He had a good idea, and he went for it. And when it ended up being a failure, he didn't have any regrets.

Four Ways Not to Be Intimidated by Failure

The pastor of the church we attend is Rick Warren. Maybe you've heard of him? He authored one of the most famous books in the world, *The Purpose Driven Life*. In one of his recent sermons, he said something about failure that stuck with me: *Fail fast and fail cheap.* What great advice! Fail fast and fail cheap. Learn how to fail in a way that's not going to bankrupt you financially, emotionally, or relationally.

Part of failing cheap can mean learning from other people's failures. Now sometimes you just have to go and screw it all up yourself in order to learn the best lessons, but there are some lessons in life you don't have to experience yourself. For example, I don't have to go out and have an affair and then watch my marriage fail in order to learn that lesson—there are plenty of people in the world who have failed in that way, and it's easy to see what the results will be. So instead of having an affair, I'm content to learn about that specific failure from other people.

Rick Warren recently said something else worth noting: when people are old, they don't regret the things they tried that didn't work out; what they regret is not taking the chance to begin with.

In other words, you don't have to be intimidated by failure! In the long run, you will not have regrets from your run-ins with failure. So here are a few things to remember that will hopefully help us fail fast, fail cheap, and not be afraid of failure.

First of all, remember that the first big failure will be the hardest. We all have plenty of small setbacks, but the first time you stick your neck out on some new venture and it flops—man, that one hurts. You put all your eggs in one basket, expecting to see a big return, and then it all falls away.

Shoot.

Yard Boys felt like my first big failure. Yes, I made a documentary. Yes, it's been seen by hundreds of thousands of people on YouTube. But it still feels like a failure, because I lost money and it didn't follow the path I wanted it to.

Immediately after that first big failure is when you'll feel most deeply the self-doubt we talked about in chapter 1—the voices will pressure you to go back to your old job, your old path, your old way of living. And it won't be just interior voices either. After that first big failure, other people will tell you you'll never get past it. If you're not careful, you'll start telling yourself that they're probably right.

What you have to remember is this: trying and (sometimes) failing will get easier. But don't give up now. Don't give up singing or writing or starting businesses. In time, you'll learn a ton of lessons from this first big failure.

Just keep going.

Remember that a good way to get to the place where failure doesn't intimidate us may sound silly, but it's not: fail even more. The more times you fail, the easier it gets to deal with it! You have to get used to the idea that failure is a distinct possibility, especially when you're out there taking big, important risks. And the more times you fail, the closer you're getting to your first big success. It's all going to help you.

I can't wait for my next big project, whether it's something on YouTube or taking *Viral* on the road or launching my next big project. But am I 100 percent positive any of these things will be huge successes? No. There's no way of knowing for sure. What I've grown to love is the challenge, the exhilaration of trying something new, and the thrill that comes with taking a risk to do something I think is important.

If any of those things fail, so be it. I'll learn lessons, become a better person, and be more likely to succeed at whatever my next project might be.

Remember to simply keep grinding. Don't even pay attention to failure. Don't give it the time of day. Get into the mentality that when you see people who have succeeded, you immediately think, *If they can do it, I can do it*, and then keep working hard. It's actually better not to be successful on your first try because you get into better habits that way—you have to keep working in spite of failure, keep grinding every single day. People who have massive successes on their first try often fall away because either they think everything they do will be that successful (and when it's not, they lose heart) or they're simply not used to working hard without seeing results.

Create a trail of consistent, hard work.

Finally, remember that sometimes things not working out can be good. Let's be real, success brings problems of its own. It can strain relationships. It can make us overly busy. It can make our lives complex and complicated.

So if you're in a phase where not everything is working out as you'd like, try to see it as a gift—as a simpler way to live or as a time that is not as busy as it might be someday. There are good things about every season in life, even when that season has some failure in it.

And you don't need me to tell you that failure in life is inevitable at some point. Every single person you come into contact with has experienced failure, some more major than others. But just because it's out there doesn't mean we have to be intimidated by it or make decisions based out of fear.

And if I can do it, you can do it. You can live your life and go after new things without being intimidated by fear.

My Biggest Failure

Yard Boys would end up being my biggest failure to date, at least if you measure it the way most people do. I spent a lot of money on it, with basically zero return (actually, I lost quite a bit). People have been super critical of it, saying we were soft, calling the documentary awful, and wondering why only one guy wanted to finish the trip.

They blamed us for ruining train hopping. Seriously.

I've never dealt with so many negative comments on something I've created. Never.

But I know I can't let the failure of *Yard Boys* intimidate me. I refuse to not do something because I'm afraid it might not work out. After all, *Yard Boys* is still a good product. People were moved by it. And there are some awesome moments and footage in it. We'll probably have more eyeballs looking at *Yard Boys* on YouTube than we would have if it was carried by one of the multi-channel networks, and I've generated new fans and made connections through it.

It always stinks to lose money and you need to be smart in your risks, but don't let failure intimidate you. Instead, make friends with it. Failure teaches you things that success can't. The more you fail, the more you learn to fail well, and you won't fail as hard next time—and you'll bounce back faster. And eventually that leads to success.

At the bottom, failure teaches you that you can fail, and you can live through it. And that knowledge alone makes failure completely worth it.

So happy failing!

CHAPTER 6

Choose Your Battles

I asked my wife, Kristin, earlier this week how she thinks I react when I hear the words, "You can't do it."

She paused and said, "Oh my gosh," and began to roll her eyes. I burst out laughing because I knew what was about to come. She went on to say, "When you hear those words, it just makes you want to do that thing a hundred times more."

I happened to be filming for a YouTube video and had my camera rolling, so she was really hamming it up for the invisible audience. (It ended up being off-topic, so it didn't make the cut.)

"Marcus is the type of person who just won't color inside the lines," she continued.

"Well," I retorted, "isn't it good to have someone who colors a little outside the lines in your life?"

She smiled. "Sometimes, sure. But . . ."

And on and on we went in a playful bantering way.

We know each other too well.

But it's true, I do have a reputation in the public eye for being someone who will challenge the conventional. My family and friends know it all too well.

Which means I am totally preaching to the choir when it comes to this next chapter.

Choose your battles.

When someone tells you, "You can't do it!" sometimes they're right.

I can't believe I just wrote that. But yes, I did. And when those rare times (at least they are rare in my head) come along, you need to know when to choose your battles and when to walk away.

I remember when I was a kid, we'd make the drive up to Pensacola to visit my great-grandfather in his old, double-wide trailer. The only thing there that looked older than the trailer was my great-grandfather—he had a massive head of slicked-back, all-white hair; a big, Squidward-looking nose; and super long, hanging ears. You know how they say your ears and nose continue to grow even after you're old? Well, if you would have seen my great-grandfather, he would have been the Wikipedia picture that comes up when you Google that factoid.

But more memorable than any of his features were his wrinkly smile and his classic, wheezy chuckle that followed every joke you never understood. But, of course, it was still funny because he laughed at it. He was like that old weeping willow tree in the Disney *Pocahontas* film.

That's it. Just imagine that.

He was such an old-timer, and he did everything the old-fashioned way. Like an old medicine man, he always told us tons of stories. He lived to be about a hundred years old, but on the day the story I'm going to tell you took place, he was probably around ninety-seven or ninety-eight.

I remember one night at his house. It was time to go to bed, and I asked for a glass of chocolate milk. It was always part of our bedtime routine when we stayed there—getting a nice glass of smooth chocolate milk. It was the kind of thing you couldn't get away with at home, but at your grandparents' house (or in this case, my great-grandparent's), the folks let it slide.

To my dismay, they brought out a small glass. I remember it was one of those small glass jars for jams.

"No, I want a big glass!" I exclaimed.

My parents probably didn't want me bouncing off the walls with all the chocolate, so they tried to convince me.

"You're not going to drink that whole thing," one of them said, pointing to the bigger glass in the cabinet.

They were right—it was massive. But I just knew I didn't want that tiny little glass.

I argued with them that I was really going to drink the whole thing.

Everyone began to laugh. They had me all riled up. But I didn't know why they thought it was so funny. Even now I don't really know, but that was my great-grandfather, laughing at jokes we didn't understand.

"Marcus," my great-grandfather said with a serious look on his face, "I bet you can't finish that huge glass in one gulp."

"I bet I can," I said.

"No way," my dad said, shaking his head and crossing his arms. "There's no way you can do that."

I should have known they were baiting me, but I was young, and after all, it was chocolate milk they were talking about. So I took the challenge and raised the glass. I chugged and chugged and chugged, and that huge glass of chocolate milk slowly drained, and I never even came up for air. It was gone.

I slammed the glass down on the table, and everyone laughed and cheered. Now I wonder if he was thinking of that old folktale where Br'er Rabbit gets the better of the fox by using reverse psychology: "Oh, please don't throw me into that briar patch!" If you have no idea what I'm talking about, just know it was written in the 1880s, and my great-grandfather loved that story. Which totally fits his rough life and sense of humor, and it is to be expected that you wouldn't get the joke because that's sort of the point.

In short, it ain't that funny.

Either way, I had done it. I had downed that huge glass of chocolate milk. I had proven them wrong. Only one problem: I suddenly didn't feel so well. My stomach was churning. I thought I might throw up.

That was a lot of chocolate milk.

Have you ever done that? Have you ever gone ahead with something just to prove people wrong?

I guess the main question I'm trying to get at is this: *Is proving people wrong always worth it?*

I can sometimes get pulled into doing things simply because someone tells me, "You can't do it."

I'll own up to that. It's true.

But there's a phrase I've been thinking about a lot lately, especially as I have to make more and more decisions about what to get involved in and what to stay out of, what brands to represent and what opportunities to pass on. And the phrase is this:

"Live to fight another day."

To me, the phrase "live to fight another day" sounds like someone barely escaping death, someone squeaking their way out of a situation, and it almost feels like it has a negative connotation. Like a failure.

But maybe it doesn't have to be that way.

I did a little bit of research on the phrase and found out

that one of the earliest uses of it dates back as far as 300 BC, but it was the novelist and poet Oliver Goldsmith who was said to have written these words:

> For he who fights and runs away
> May live to fight another day;
> But he who is in battle slain
> Can never rise and fight again.[7]

It's really the perfect metaphor for us as creative people, isn't it?

Sometimes someone will tell you, "You can't do it," and you'll fight so hard to win that one battle and prove them wrong that you're left with nothing after that. You did it, sure, but after all the work, you're burned-out. And maybe you missed another, better opportunity. You didn't survive to fight another day, because you're finished.

You certainly didn't win the war.

I'm thinking that sometimes admitting you can't do something (for whatever reason) is the more strategic thing to do.

Sometimes? Walking away is the win.

Getting Arrested

There's something I didn't tell you in the last chapter about the end of our train adventure. We started that whole thing, or at least I did, with this huge goal of getting across the United States, going all the way from Los Angeles to New York City, and I really wanted to make it. Everyone was telling us it was nearly an impossibility if you tried to do it by yourself.

But going with a group of five guys?

Forget it.

"You'll stand out too much. Someone will see you eventually. You'll get caught—you'll never make it the entire way."

And you know what? They were right. Because there were five of us, it was super hard to hide, to stay out of sight. It was tough boarding the trains efficiently too, because we were all scrambling and running and we had all that gear. And of course whenever you're traveling in a group, everything takes way longer, and you can't just make snap decisions. But while jumping trains, that's the name of the game: snap decisions. So the fact that we made it as far as we did was pretty great.

We ended up finally get caught because we got careless, hanging off the side of the train and just enjoying ourselves instead of focusing on staying hidden. A railroad worker saw us and called ahead, so by the time we got to the next stop, the police were waiting for us.

And in case you're wondering, that wasn't a good feeling.

I seriously considered running. Believe me. It would have been easy to jump off the train and dart into the woods before they got to the train. But not all of us were ready, and a few of the guys were at the opposite end of the fifty-three-foot-long cargo car we were riding. I had no way of talking to them, and they weren't paying attention. I was so tempted to take off, but I couldn't leave my friends there. So, sadly, the captain went down with the ship, and we all went along with the police.

The ride in the car was foreboding and silent, and I could tell a few of the guys were completely freaking out. I guess I was a little bit too—*What were they going to do to us? Put us in jail? Would we be sharing a holding cell with real criminals? How long could they leave us there? What was I going to tell my parents?* The whole thing felt uncertain and more than a little scary.

"So, what's the process from here?" I asked one of the officers, trying to sound nonchalant, but there was anxiety in my voice.

"You guys'll get booked into jail and charged with trespassing, and then you can either bail out or wait and see the judge in the morning. If you wait to see the judge in the morning, you'll get fed twice." He said that last part ironically and ended it with a smoker's cough that sounded like one of his lungs was coming up. We glanced at each other. I didn't even want to think about spending the night in jail.

It turned out the whole deal was less tense than I thought it was going to be. They stuck us in a cell for a while; we paid bail; and then we went and stayed at a hotel—the beautiful Venture Motor Inn—and took our first shower in weeks. We stayed the night because we had to go before the judge in the morning.

The main thing that happened that night was that we started talking about whether or not we should keep going. We were pretty sure this first arrest wouldn't result in anything serious, but we also didn't know what the consequences might be if we were caught again. What would a second arrest look like on our permanent records? None of us wanted this little adventure to turn into something with far-reaching negative consequences. Especially for the other guys who were pursuing traditional jobs where a "criminal record" would hurt them.

I talked to my dad that night on the phone.

"Guess what? We went to jail," I said with a wry grin on my face.

"Well, you've got a long way to go," he replied. "What are you going to do? What happens if you get a second offense?"

"We're going to check into it," I said. "But the guys are already saying they're not sure if they want to finish it or not."

"Yeah, if you get caught again . . ." my mom said quietly, her voice trailing off. "You don't want to go to jail, honey."

The last thing I wanted to do was give up. I hate quitting, and in this instance, I had planned for so long to make this trip happen. I had learned everything I thought I could learn about hopping trains. I wanted to prove to everyone, including my friends, that we could do it. That night was one of the hardest nights of the whole trip for me, lying there in bed, staring up at a dark ceiling. To think we were on the edge of this whole thing being over so suddenly.

Should we keep going, or should we hang it up and live to fight another day?

When You Should Quit

I think a lot of people are like me, and maybe the other half, when they hear no, they nod their head, agree, and quit. Unless it's something I don't care about, I rarely think, *Yeah, I'm just going to let this one go.* I don't like hearing no. I don't like hearing, "You can't do this." And so sometimes, in the face of that, I'll push and push and push.

But I know I have to learn when to say no, when to run away, so that I can fight another day. There's a wisdom that comes with maturity.

So how do we know when we should listen to that wiser inner voice and say no? How do we know when pushing forward is going to do nothing but burn us out, defeat us, and set us up for more losses?

I have a few thoughts, though admittedly, I still work this out on a case-by-case basis. And I'm not sure these four things are all we need to consider when we're thinking about choosing our battles and living to fight another day. But maybe they can be a good jumping off point for your own thinking.

Remember you're not the only one. There are a lot of times in this fast-paced, dog-eat-dog world of social media influencers and the entertainment business where I feel like I could really push my representatives, agents, or managers to do more. There are a lot of times when I'm tempted to apply a lot of pressure, get upset at the results, and ask why they're not able to make a particular deal or opportunity work or what's taking so long with this project or why is this person I know getting all these deals when it's not working out for me in the moment?

In other words, there are a lot of times when I'm tempted to just chew them out. To be over-the-top and vent my frustrations.

It's true.

There are so many situations where I feel like I need to have a "real talk" with the people I work with, but guess what?

A lot of times it's worth it just to keep quiet. Sometimes I have to simply accept that something didn't work out and remember that it's not all about me. My perspective isn't the only one.

I sometimes find myself in this situation when it comes to sponsored posts. Some brands have specific talking points that are just so unrealistic.

And sometimes it feels so robotic.

I think to myself, *I do not sound like that.*

I would never say those words.

Why am I doing this?

I start to wonder how long until people are saying, "Marcus Johns is a sellout."

It makes me want to fight it and say, "No way, this is ridiculous," but I know if I push back too hard, I'll blow up the entire deal.

Instead of fighting it, instead of making a big fuss, instead of burning bridges, I do what they ask. I post the picture. Write the caption. Include the hashtag. Because at the end of the day, if I know that the brand or product is something that is worth the partnership for the future, then it is worthwhile. My opinion about whatever specific thing we're doing isn't the only one.

The main thing I have to ask myself is this: Am I fine with representing this? If that checks out, then I'm not going to blow up the deal just because I have to include some clunky language and details about the product in the post.

Remember, you can't do everything. One of the most important times we need to live to fight another day is when we start to feel like we're being pulled in a thousand different directions.

When I started working on my musical, social media had to take a back seat. I was producing, writing, and preparing to play the lead role, and doing social media full-time was something I did not have the bandwidth to be successful at both.

You can't do everything. And sometimes it will feel like a rough trade-off. You'll have to say no to things you love to do.

It wasn't easy for me to pull away from social media. I had a lot of fears and questions about whether my audience would hang around if I wasn't posting every day or every week or every month.

And it seemed like a crazy trade-off. I tried to put on

the performance of my life for a thousand people instead of making videos that could have been viewed by a million people. One thousand people could see my show and go, "Wow! That's amazing!" or one million people could see my work and say, "Yeah, that was pretty good. I like that. I'll watch the next video in my feed."

But that's the trade-off, and for that period of time I would rather give a thousand people an unforgettable, in-person experience. To me, that was worth a million online impressions. There's value in seeing people face-to-face—people who are cued in and focused on what I was doing—instead of stumbling onto something I made after watching a gardening video. Or whatever.

When you say no to something, when you decide you're going to live to fight another day, there's always a trade-off.

Always.

Just make sure you know what you're trading.

Consider the regrets you might have. When I had the idea of creating the musical and had to decide if I was willing to put aside my social media videos for a time, one thing that helped a lot was thinking about which I would regret more.

Would I regret it if I did the musical and stepped back from my YouTube stuff, taking a break from making videos and engaging online?

Or would I regret it if I continued to focus on social media and decided not to do the musical? What about all of the new relationships I would make with fun-loving, creative people? What about all the experience I would gain?

Thinking about it that way made it easy for me. I knew I would always regret it if I didn't give the musical a shot. So that made the decision easy. I knew I'd have to say no to social media for a while.

I had to choose my battles.

Consider the consequences. Sometimes when we're trying to decide if we should just say no to something so we can live to fight another day, what we really need to do is just be honest with ourselves.

Because a lot of times we know that this thing we're tempted to try is not going to be good for us. Maybe we know it's going to demand way too much time, more than what we have to give. Or maybe we know that if we say yes, it's going to pull us in a direction we don't want to go.

Or maybe we know it's just not good for us.

You know, sort of like chugging an entire large glass of chocolate milk when you're a kid. You know it's going to taste good going down, but you also know it's not going to do you any favors.

I think we run into opportunities like this all the time—things that grab our attention or sound interesting or look like they might be fun—but deep inside, we know we should say no or take others' advice around us. We know it's not going to end well.

We know that drinking that entire glass is going to give us a bad stomachache.

We need to be honest with ourselves so we can live to fight another day.

Saying No Is Not Failure

So there we were, trying to decide to push it or to choose our battles and walk away from this train ride.

What did I say into the camera?

"I know I'm the only person who wants to keep going. I wish we would have gotten caught in Chicago or somewhere in Pennsylvania, where we don't have much further to go. But there's such a far distance to travel, and I know everyone else wants to give up, and I'm so upset because we didn't hit our goal."

We all sat on the bed in one of the motel rooms and hashed it out.

And we decided we weren't going any farther.

It hurt. It was hard. I hated to turn back.

But it was definitely our chance to live to fight another day.

There's something I want to end this chapter with. Something that's important as you start thinking about how to do this great big thing you're about to do. This is it. Are you ready?

Saying no isn't the same thing as failing.

I know a lot of times there's a ton of pressure to do certain things. Maybe you're feeling like the world is telling you that you should start a blog or a YouTube channel or a podcast. Maybe you're feeling the pressure to go back to school or take certain classes.

Whatever it is—whatever other people are asking you to do or whatever you feel like you "should" do—remember . . . saying no isn't the same thing as failing.

When I said no to opportunities that came up while I was writing my musical, those weren't failures; those were examples of me choosing my battles. When I first got married and had to step back from some of my creative endeavors to focus on my new life with Kristin, that wasn't me failing at work; that was me stepping back so I could fight another day.

When you start to think hard about whether or not to say no, it's so important to remember the bigger picture as to why you do the things you do. It's not just about pursuing originality or self-importance. It's not just about follower numbers or padding your bank account. Ultimately, what we do, we have to do out of love—for ourselves, for those around us, for God.

Don't be afraid to say no.

You have a long, creative path ahead of you.

Think carefully about the things you are saying yes to.

Choose your battles.

CHAPTER 7

Take Courage

My dad is dope. For many reasons.

First of all, he's the fire chief for the Palm Beach County Fire Department.

Second, he's very wise.

Third, he gets it done. Gets what done? Anything. Need it finished? Today? And you have no budget? No problem. He has a way of solving problems and can somehow just get his way with people. He commands negotiations super well, and when he asks for something, he gets it. I don't know what it is about him that makes people listen to him all the time.

It's actually kind of weird to see how much respect he commands, even though he's not like a six foot five movie star with a wide grin and charismatic appearance. He's like five foot eight, and my mom sometimes says he kind of looks like the Geico lizard—if that lizard was a man, with short legs and a long torso. There's nothing about him physically that makes you think, *I have to listen to this guy.*

Except he still manages to have a way about him that inspires confidence in everyone.

It's hard to explain other than saying, "He just gets it done."

One thing my dad always says, which I absolutely love,

is this: "I can think of ten bad ideas before you can think of one good one." It's kind of a humble brag, but it also reflects someone who doesn't care what other people think of him, who's willing to throw ideas out there and try them—whether or not they work doesn't really matter.

Oh, and there's also this—my dad can fix anything. He knows a little bit about everything. He's wise, and he's not confrontational. He's one of these people you just don't want to let down. You know how you have those friends you never upset because you're kind of scared about what would happen if you did?

That's my dad. But not in a scary way. You just don't want to disappoint him.

I don't command the same amount of respect my dad does—maybe it's my age, or maybe it's my personality, but you wouldn't even think of taking advantage of my dad. You don't want to see where that road leads. Part of that is because he's been around the block.

One of the greatest compliments I ever received from my dad was when I was talking to him about the musical.

"Marcus," he said, "it's very impressive that you're able to get everyone to listen to you and direct the show at the same time, while having all the creative ideas and acting in the show. You're good at leading a crowd and juggling things."

"Well, Dad," I said, "you're the same way."

We were specifically reminiscing on a moment during the musical when one of the legs had broken on a pivotal set piece. The actor who was supposed to be pushing it out during the next scene freaked out because he broke it. Thankfully my dad was backstage helping at the time and managed to fix it in about thirty seconds. We were laughing at the reenactment my dad gave of the actor who was so worked up by the broken leg.

He said, "I've put out a lot of fires, so now when I'm out doing something else, when people get flustered and lose it, I just think, *Dude, the building's not on fire.*"

The building's not on fire.

What a perfect thing to remember when you're feeling stressed and overwhelmed. When my dad is putting out a fire in a burning building, there are actual lives at stake—the people who live and work there, the lives of his crew, and the lives of people passing by. It's a literal ticking time bomb. He has to put out that fire and make quick decisions that will save lives and property, and he has to live with the decisions he makes on the spot. He can't reverse the things he does. He has to go with it.

He's learned to do that, to make hard decisions, in the most heightened, crazy way. I think that's why he has such command over a room—he's been putting out literal fires for thirty years. When you've been tested in life at the highest level possible, everything else becomes so much easier. I think that's the most important thing: *experience.* It has a huge impact on your ability and your confidence level. My dad, because of his experience, has the ability to be a calm leader and manager.

I want to become that. I want people to trust me to put out life's fires.

Why are we stressed-out about lighting? Why are we losing sleep over the venue? Why are we worried about how many tickets we'll sell or views our video will get or how much money this brand is going to offer?

It's all going to be fine.

We can build our confidence from that one phrase.

The building's not on fire.

When you've been tested, you know things aren't that bad. And when you know that, then you know you can do it.

I could go on and on about my dad, but I have to tell you one more story about him, because it's the perfect "you can't do it" illustration of acting with confidence. There are times when you have to have confidence in yourself, bet all the chips on your decision, and not let other people's opinions or thoughts make you second-guess yourself.

This was one of those times, and I got to see my dad in action.

Whenever my dad visits us in California, we go to Home Depot because we have, like, eight projects lined up between my brother's house and mine. We usually have rooms to paint and lighting fixtures to switch out, and then there's the shed to build off the back of the garage.

You know, that kind of stuff.

Anyway, we were working on a shed and had to make a run to Home Depot, and as we're driving there, we began to see black smoke billowing not too far in the distance.

"Yeah, that's a car fire," my dad said, and he pointed out how he could tell it had just started. The smoke was doing a certain thing, which meant a certain thing, and he was getting all expert on it. Soon we were one light away, and we could see it. And my dad was right—it was a car fire, right there on the side of the road. But there were no flashing lights.

"Looks like we're going to beat the fire department," my dad said, looking up and down the street, expecting to hear the sirens any minute.

"Dad," I said, pulling out my phone to start making a video, "you should totally put it out."

He's like, "No, I'll let the young guys do it."

After some convincing, he agreed. "Well, if we beat them there, why not?"

We pulled up and were the first ones on the scene.

We got out of our car, and I could see flames coming out from under the hood. It looked like it was close to catching the interior of the car on fire too. That's when we had another crazy realization.

The car was literally parked directly in front of a fire station.

I'm not even kidding.

And the fire truck wasn't in the garage bay.

It was all so ironic. "Dad, you *have* to do it," I insisted again.

There was another guy standing there who had been riding by on his bike when the car started burning. "Shoot," he said, "it's on fire."

That was it. That was all he had to offer. Master of the obvious.

Meanwhile, my dad looked around for a hose, and this other guy ran around the side of a nearby house and pulled a hose around, but it didn't reach, so my dad told him to look for another one that they could add to it. They found one and connected it, and my dad started walking calmly over to the car fire.

That's when the police officers showed up.

"Hey, man, you can't put out the fire like that."

My dad turned toward them, and of course that day he was wearing his Palm Beach Fire Rescue T-shirt.

He said in a super calm voice, "Oh yeah I can."

He was so calm, and I was freaking out—a car was on fire; the police were telling him he couldn't put it out; and all we had was a garden hose. But that didn't stop my dad.

I think my dad's calm demeanor sort of caught the cops off guard.

"You can't put out a car fire with a garden hose," they kept saying, but it was clear they weren't going to do anything to stop my dad, so he got to work. Besides, he was older than they were, and why would they stop someone from putting out a fire? That wouldn't make any sense.

"I've seen this before," one of the cops said. "There's no way you can put out that fire. You need the fire department."

But Dad wasn't paying any attention, not anymore.

At this point, they had noticed the firefighter shirt and had given up trying to prove him wrong.

My dad was acting with courage. He knew what had to be done, and he was doing it. He grabbed the hood and lifted it open with his bare hands while flames where blasting through the grill.

Just like that. Sometimes you just have to have the courage to go for it.

Finding the Courage

Sometimes you'll lose faith in yourself. Sometimes other people will be telling you no. Maybe you're coming off a huge failure.

None of that matters.

But, Marcus, I just don't know if I have the courage I need.

No problem. I've got six things that help me find the courage I need to make big things happen—like putting out fires and acting on dreams and goals.

1. Remember that you know what you know. You'll run into a lot of people who have authority and who are used to wielding their authority over others. They're used to putting up roadblocks, and they're used to people listening to whatever they say. Just like the police officers in the story of my dad putting out the car fire with a garden hose, they will want to tell you what's up. What works. What doesn't.

But when you remember that you know what you know, then you can have the courage to keep going—no matter what these "experts" have to say. A lot of these people have some kind of a badge or name tag or a formal position of authority, and they are more than willing to tell you what can't be done. They're the gatekeepers in the industry you're trying to work in. But what they don't know is how badly you want it—they are used to running into people who will hear what they have to say and then give up easily. But you know how much you want it. You know how hard you've worked. And your unique experience has prepared you for this.

You know what you know. Just like my dad did, don't let other people talk you out of that.

2. Get past the easy no. This goes along with that last one, because a lot of times the people in authority will not only give you the quick no because they can't be bothered, but they'll also encourage the voice of doubt in yourself. They are used to telling people no all day long, and 99 percent of the people they say no to simply take it and walk away. Getting past that easy no in your own mind may take some work. It may be hard. You may have to oppose the person in power at times, or ask to talk to the manager—yes, you may have to be that person! You may have to do the annoying thing and keep pressing. But first you'll have to get past your own self-doubt. So don't let your own initial, easy no turn you off!

3. Don't set mediocre goals. Most people live mediocre lives because they're setting mediocre goals. What does a mediocre goal look like? Usually a mediocre goal is someone else's that you decided to make your own. For them, it may be a good one, but when you take on other people's goals, they almost always end up being, for you, mediocre. It's not what you need. Big, amazing goals are formed when you stop looking at what other people need, what other people believed possible, and start thinking about what *you* need to do, what *you* want to do, and what's possible for *you*!

For a lot of people, being a YouTuber is a mediocre goal. I really think so. Most of the great YouTubers have lives and careers and passions, and they only happen to have a YouTube channel. But when someone's sole goal is to be a YouTuber and they have content without an actual life, it's a mediocre goal.

Stop looking around at the goals other people are setting and making them yours. Stop setting mediocre goals. Start creating original goals that seem a little crazy, maybe a little impossible, and don't be afraid to go after what you know, deep down, you need to do.

4. Be willing to build it from the ground up. Think about 3-D printers for a moment. Have you seen these things? They take any plan you put in them, any model of anything, and spit out a three-dimensional plastic model of whatever it was you put in. A lot of people are just like those printers. They take other people's ideas, code them, and regurgitate them.

But as human beings, we have the ability to be more creative than that. I say, grab the clay and mold it yourself. Imperfections and all. Be a part of the process!

What's stopping most people from creating their own amazing things, projects, or products that are actually going to change the world or change our perspectives or be something that's not just mediocre?

Isn't it usually just that they're afraid of the work it takes to design something new? I think most of us are intimidated by the idea of starting from the ground up. Too often we think, wouldn't it be great to write a musical or a script or a book, but the problem is that we frame it in comparison to other already utilized ideas—*Wouldn't it be great if there was another* Spiderman *movie?*

But success doesn't come when we replicate what others have done; success is a personal discovery! That's when success happens–when we're doing something new and discovering it for ourselves. I build small gas engines for motorcycles, but soon I may decide to try to build a motorcycle, and then I may try to build a car, and then maybe a house, and then a neighborhood, and then, you know, maybe a floating city in the ocean. Sometimes you can find the courage you need by starting with your own original drive, whatever it is you want to contribute or to see in the world, and build it from the ground up.

5. Know what the secret sauce is. The secret sauce, the shortcut to end all shortcuts, the one thing you need to know that will magically advance you to success is this: there is no secret sauce.

There isn't.

There are a million books out there trying to tell you differently, and just as many Facebook ads promising all kinds of incredible things that have to do with money and power and success, but you can't believe them, because there is no secret. There is no one thing you can do.

No one thing you're missing out on.

No password.

No shortcuts.

For many of us, this can be incredibly disappointing.

We just want someone to tell us what to do, and we want it to be quick, and we want it to be painless! But that's not how it works.

The road to success is long and there's a lot of hard work involved.

There is no secret sauce.

6. Remember that the building is not on fire! Sometimes we lose our courage because we think our lives depend on getting this next thing right. And most of the time our lives and others' lives do not depend on it. And knowing that, we can find the courage to take a chance and try things that might not work. It wouldn't be the end of the world. Another way to remember this is to ask, *What's the worst that could happen?* Actually think that through, and even if it happened, is it that bad? This work you're doing, this business you're creating, this musical you're composing, this piece of art you're working on . . . if you fail, will the world end? Will the sun not go on rising? Is it a life-and-death issue?

Maybe the building is not on fire. Go from there.

Car Fire Hero

So the cops were watching. The fire truck was nowhere to be found. My dad started by spraying water up under the car, and he explained it to me the entire time—what he was doing, why he was doing it, where he was spraying the water, and how that would help extinguish the fire quickly. Meanwhile, the cops removed themselves to the other side of the street and stood there with their arms crossed.

Dad put out the fire in, like, forty-five seconds.

Here's the thing—my dad knew what he knew, and he wasn't going to let anyone, no matter how smug (even if they were cops), tell him otherwise. He had been putting out fires for decades.

The police officers sort of ambled by as they left the scene.

"I guess you proved me wrong," the officer said. Dad just looked at him and smiled.

That's when the fire truck pulled up. I guess the fire crew was out on another call, but who really knows. All that mattered was the fire was out and they were too late.

The firefighting vigilante had struck.

Seriously. It was too perfect. I have a video of all of this happening, and I want to go back and edit it so that Dad drops the hose like a mic and walks off, and then the screen goes black, with the words "Thug Life" illuminated in white.

So maybe the building's not on fire—just a car is.

And sometimes you're just a garden hose away from eternal glory.

All you need is to find your courage and let it rip.

CHAPTER 8

Trust Your Gut

What do you do when your intuition is telling you one thing but people are encouraging you to do something else?

Do you go with your instincts, or do you try to make decisions "more rationally"?

We had less than two weeks of rehearsal time to prepare for the musical. It was a huge group of actors, musicians, and stage crew, all working on the same super compressed time frame.

So you can imagine how I felt when we were a few days in, staring down the barrel of less than two weeks until opening night, and one of our lead characters dropped out because he had booked a role in a movie. How would we find someone to take his place? I mean, technically I could have made him stay with the show, but I couldn't bring myself to enforce the contract he had signed. What was I going to do—tell him he couldn't go be in a movie because he had signed on to be in my musical? That would have been messed up, and besides, I didn't want people around who were wishing they were somewhere else.

The next day I made the announcement in front of the whole company that, sadly, he would be leaving because he got a big opportunity, and we all wished him luck.

But what were we going to do without him? Who could we find to take his place with so little time remaining?

There was only one guy who came to mind. He was the guy who on paper did not fit the character at all. During his audition, he had acted, sang, and looked the exact opposite of how I described the character to casting. But somehow during the audition, his performance made me think of the character in a completely new light—who the character could be.

It's easy to see someone audition for a role and say, "We should definitely choose them because of their résumé and the strength of their singing voice, plus they look the part." But sometimes I was drawn to someone without knowing why. I just knew they had the right essence of the character. I really couldn't explain it to the other people who had input on casting. The casting director or producer would argue on behalf of one person, often even someone who on the surface made more sense, but it just didn't feel right to me. Sometimes we went with their choice, and sometimes we went with my gut.

Part of the reason my casting people and I didn't always see eye to eye, I'm sure, was that I had been thinking about these characters for years. They were real people to me, and I intuitively knew more about who they were than anyone else. I had written them. I had thought them up. I had a certain connection. I couldn't always articulate what it was that made a certain actor right for a given part.

I just knew it. In my gut.

In this case, I ended up getting the guy I had originally been drawn to because the casting director's first choice had to leave. The guy getting a second chance was the guy who got explained away. But this time it worked out.

You know what?

My intuition was right, even though I hadn't listened to it at first. He worked out really well in the part.

You always wonder about the "what ifs" in life. What if I made the wrong decision? What if I would have gone in a different direction? In this case I got to live out both scenarios, and although both were great choices, the outcome reinforced my confidence in going with my gut.

Some choices in life don't carry with them lifelong consequences. The casting of the musical was obviously important to me, but it wouldn't necessarily alter the rest of my life (at least as far as I know!).

But there are other times when your decision on whether or not to trust your gut can change the trajectory of your entire life!

There was this one time when trusting my gut really paid off.

It had to do with a girl named Kristin.

The whole thing started when I was driving home to Palm Beach with my sister, Shelby, for winter break. We were returning from college in Tallahassee, where we both attended Florida State, and it was a great day—the semester was over, and Christmas was almost here. I can still remember passing by the Gainesville exits in my sister's 2000 Hyundai Elantra, windows down, both of us soaking in the cold air. That's when my sister took out her phone and started Snapchatting with one of her friends, just doing her thing, and I glanced over out of curiosity.

I saw her for the first time, this girl on my sister's cell phone making a silly face. She had big eyes and a beautiful smile. That picture has been erased forever, gone, a fleeting moment, but it's still stuck in my head.

Wow, I thought to myself, *that girl is beautiful*.

I glanced at Shelby.

"Who is that?" I asked, trying to sound nonchalant.

"Her name's Kristin. She goes to my Bible study."

And they kept chatting back and forth, and I saw another picture of Kristin. The two of them were just goofing off. Shelby held out the phone to take a photo of the two of us to send back to Kristin.

"Hold up," I said, because my hair was all funky and I didn't want her to see me like that. And in that moment, I had an epiphany—I released videos to millions of people every day with insane faces and purposely messed-up hair, yet I cared about how I look for this random girl on Snapchat I didn't even know? I might not have cared what anyone else in the world thought, but as Shelby held out her phone, I cared about how I would look when this girl saw me.

I liked this girl.

"I want to meet that girl," I said.

"No way," Shelby replied. "Really?"

"Yeah," I said. "What's she like?"

When Shelby realized that I was showing interest in her friend, she totally started playing her up. "Oh, Kristin? She's the best." And she went on and on.

"What's her voice like?" I asked, already trying to imagine what she was like. I already had this picture of her and how we would be together. It was the strangest thing, an immediate connection.

A gut feeling.

"Her voice?" Shelby asked, uncertain how to respond, because she didn't want to say anything that would eliminate my interest in her friend.

"Yeah, is her voice a high voice or deep, or . . . ?"

"It's kind of not too high," she hedged, "but it's not too deep. It's kind of in the middle."

"I was kind of imagining that she has a high-pitched voice. I've always liked girls with high, feminine voices," I said, and Shelby cut me off.

"It's the highest-pitch voice I've ever heard."

I laughed, but I knew I had to meet Kristin. I couldn't stop thinking about her all through winter break. There was something about her, something different, something that clicked. Again, I had this gut feeling that she was the one for me.

Shelby had arranged for us to meet at church on the first Sunday back from break, which was a little awkward because by then word had gotten back to her that I liked her and wanted to meet her. We ended up going out to lunch together, along with my sister and their whole group of friends. I sat diagonally across from Kristin. I didn't want to sit right across from her—duh, that would be way too forward—and if I sat next to her, I couldn't have a natural conversation. Needless to say, I was so nervous! And I rarely get nervous. Later, Kristin would tell me we only had one exchange during the entire lunch.

"That's a nice purse," I said.

"Oh, thank you," she replied. "My aunt gave it to me."

"Wow," I said. "Your aunt must be really nice."

Seriously.

Your aunt must be really nice?

That was the best I could do?

What a dummy!

After that lunch, I told Shelby I needed another chance, so two days later, she said she was going out to get ice cream with Kristin and I was welcome to come along. I met up with Shelby, Kristin, and another friend at Bruster's Ice Cream.

There we got to talk with a bit less of a crowd, and we told each other all kinds of funny stories and made each other laugh a lot. It was fun, and I thought it went well. Kristin later told me that after that night, she thought I was the funniest guy she had ever met. So I definitely killed it.

See, guys?

Gut feelings.

All joking aside, it's really strange to think back on those early days with Kristin because now I know her so well. But then I didn't. It's hard to imagine us barely knowing each other, wondering where it was all leading.

During the course of the conversation, it came up that Shelby and her friend group were going to a well-known youth conference. The only problem was that Kristin was the only one who wasn't going because she hadn't gotten a ticket before they sold out.

"Oh, I can get you a ticket, no problem," I said, acting like I knew people who could get us tickets, even though I definitely did not know anyone who could get us tickets.

I had no idea how I was going to do it.

"You can get me a ticket?" she said, excitedly.

"Sure. And I'm going too."

Except I wasn't going. Or hadn't been planning on going. But now I was definitely going, so I needed to find *two* tickets— one for me and one for Kristin—because I really wanted to spend time with her, and going to this conference together seemed like a great opportunity for that.

Figuring out how to get her a ticket became my one goal in life.

I immediately went to Twitter and begged.

"Does anyone have two tickets to this conference? I'm desperate."

I ended up sourcing two tickets from a stranger on Twitter, but I had to pick up the tickets there, at the venue in Atlanta. So when we left and headed north, I still didn't actually have the tickets in my possession. Kristin was meeting us there in another car, so had this Twitter meetup not worked out, she would have gotten all the way there and had nothing to do for two days.

Even worse, I had terrible gas. Was it nerves? Was it something I ate? Was it a curse from God? I have never had it like I did that day. Fortunately, Kristin thought it was her friend who was with us, and I didn't say anything to make her think otherwise.

"Oh my word, Megan!" Kristin kept saying, and even after her friend denied it. "Whatever!" My gas was so smelly and bad that when we recently reminisced on the conference and our first extended time together, she actually brought up how her friend had the worst gas that day. I broke the news to her that it was me the whole time.

My gas was that unforgettable!

Seriously I'm surprised it took so many years for her to make that connection. I could have sworn I told her about it before.

Anyway, we made it to the conference; I got the tickets; and most importantly, I got Kristin's phone number.

Maybe you're wondering what this story has to do with gut feelings, instincts, and intuition? Well, from the first moment I saw Kristin on Snapchat, I pretty much knew she was the one. And I actually told her that soon after we met—on our first date, one week after the conference.

It was the first time we'd had a chance to sit down and talk to each other alone, and I told her, in my stereotypically goofy way, "We are totally going to get married."

She opened her mouth wide and laughed. "Okay."

But even though I said it in a funny way, I was completely serious. I meant it. I had a calm assurance about her—that she was the one for me.

"I'm serious," I said. "I only date people with the intention of getting married. We'll get married, of course, and probably have three kids."

She just smiled. I don't think she knew what to say.

After that, I kept joking with her about it. "You know, I'll probably move to LA by the end of this semester, but that's okay because we can get married and you can move to California with me and I'll pay for the rest of your college."

Ah, the plans I had!

Well, the first part of that came true within a few months. I did move to LA.

We dated for three months in person before I moved away. But she stayed in Tallahassee for nearly three years in order to finish her degree.

Talk about a gut feeling being tested!

It would have been easy to take a break, to convince myself that maybe it wasn't the right time. But I had made up my mind. I knew what I knew, and I was going to fight for our relationship, our future.

Kristin and I recently binged all the seasons of *Shark Tank*. If you don't know, *Shark Tank* is a television show in which people present their new business ideas and hope one of these billionaires will invest in their dream.

One of my favorite things to do is create new ideas and business opportunities, so it's one of my favorite shows—I just love seeing all these creative people who are trying to get their new businesses off the ground. They fight so hard and have to compromise with the sharks if they want to make their dreams come true.

As an investor on the show, Kevin O'Leary (along with the others) has to crunch numbers and gauge how confident he is in the various businesses and the people running them. But even once they've answered all of his financial questions, he still has to make a decision based on his gut instinct. And he has an awesome quote that sort of encapsulates trusting your gut, instincts, and intuition: "Trusting your gut is not an emotion. It's an index of risk, a barometer of experience."[8]

I love that quote because O'Leary is getting at the heart of what makes our intuition so important: it's not a random feeling or emotion; it's actually our way of determining how much risk is involved based on our previous life experiences.

A lot of people, including my closest friends and even my dad, have often remarked that I have really good gut instincts.

"You need to follow your gut," my dad has told me, "because when you do, great things normally happen."

He's right. When I think back through my life, pretty much all of my biggest successes have happened because I trusted my gut. Not because I tediously studied the analytics of every option during my endeavors, but simply because I had a sense that there was something I needed to do, something I thought would work out, and then I gave it my best.

Yet "gut instinct" is such a hard thing to quantify. What does it even mean—trusting your gut? How can we break it down into something tangible? Because it's not "just a feeling." Like O'Leary says, trusting your gut is an "index of risk," a "barometer of experience." In other words, when your gut is telling you to do something, it's because you know something you can't articulate, and that something you know is based on your experiences, your awareness, and your mind doing calculations that you're not even conscious of.

In a *Psychology Today* article by Al Pittampalli titled "When Should You Trust Your Gut? Here's What the Science Says," he writes that "humans are constantly scanning their environment, trying to detect familiar situations." In other words, our brains are always looking for things we've experienced before and quickly making calculations about what the future is going to hold, based on how those experiences worked out in the past. In fact, Pittampalli goes on to cite Gary Klein's book *Sources of Power* and says there are four specific kinds of information our brains are searching for all the time. They are relevant cues, expectancies, plausible goals, and typical actions.[9]

Relevant cues. In the middle of all the things going on around us, everything we can see and smell and hear, our minds are sifting through it, looking for things that are meaningful and then using that meaningful information to suggest what we should do next. This is the beginning of a gut instinct. I mean, when I was making Vines, a lot of the time it felt random to me—I would get this sense that I should make a video about something, and it seemed to come out of nowhere. It seemed like it was intuition. And it was, but it was actually my brain remembering what worked in the past, sensing that something similar was going to happen, and then triggering me to make a video. The more I did this, the better I got and the more followers I had. I called it a gut instinct, but it all started with my brain subconsciously identifying cues that made sense to me.

Expectancies. This is the second kind of information our brains are scouring the world around us for. In other words, it takes the relevant cues and then works out what we should expect to happen. Going back to my Vine example, when I had a gut feeling that I should make a video based on relevant cues, my brain immediately began calculating the possibility of whether or not that video idea would resonate with my followers.

Plausible goals. Intuition, after identifying the relevant cues and what I expect to happen, starts spitting out things I might want to happen, things I might want to have: *This video could get a million views on YouTube. This video could make my friends and family laugh. This video could work with a brand deal.* All of these goals and ideas are part of the gut feeling on whether or not to make the video.

Typical actions. After my mind cycles through all of those things in a split second, intuition will suggest what to do. Maybe my gut feeling about a potential video is that it won't do well—I'll back off from the idea and let it be. But if my instinct is that it's a strong idea, intuition will move me forward into creating it, and intuition will continue with me through the entire idea, leading me to tweak this or that, change this or that, add this or that. It all happens so fast that we write it off as "just a gut feeling." But my brain in a small way did a very complex equation. It recalled an index of analytics based on successful videos and gave me the green light to post that particular idea.

Amazing, isn't it? Maybe you used to think gut instinct was just some pie-in-the-sky excuse people gave for doing what they wanted to do and not listening to the evidence. Yet our brains are constantly calculating where our current experiences are most likely to lead us, using these four cues.

Can you begin to understand why you should maybe start trusting your gut instincts a bit more?

How to Build Up Your Intuition

It may seem like a simple fact of nature that some people have good intuition, while others do not. But there are actually things you can do to become more intuitive and develop your gut instincts to a place where you can trust where they're leading you.

Here are a just a few practices the experts recommend to help you develop your intuition:

Get quality practice.[10] The most important part of developing our gut instincts is gaining experience in the area where we'd like to use our gut more often. This is super hard in the beginning because it's like jumping on a train when you've never done it before. You just have to keep doing it—that's the only way you'll get good at it. If you want to develop your gut instinct, you have to be willing to try and fail and try and fail and try again, because in all of those experiences, your mind is honing its intuitive ability.

Use it more frequently over time.[11] Recent experiments and studies have shown that not only is quality practice important in growing our intuition, but it's also crucial that we do it a lot, and that we do it a lot over a long period of time. Joel Pearson, the lead researcher of a study published in *Psychological Science*, said, "It's all about learning to use unconscious information in your brain."[12] In the same way you can become more confident in your decision making when you get used to using logic and reasoning, you can also learn to trust your intuition if you use it more often over long periods of time.

Eliminate anxiety.[13] It seems like more and more people suffer from anxiety, and it's getting more prevalent with each generation. With the way the media works—negative attention driving the most clicks, and social media breeding an endless system of comparison—no wonder everyone is stressing out. But there's something unexpected that all of this fear is causing: "Anxiety, researchers discovered, can effectively silence our gut instincts."

In a study where groups were given either information that made them feel happy and secure or information that made them feel anxious and on edge, the first group performed much better at intuitive tasks than the latter. You can at least be aware that the time to make calls that require you to listen to your gut isn't when you're feeling most anxious about the situation. Calming down by going for a run, hanging out with friends, or counting your blessings is probably a better foundation for getting in touch with your intuition than late-night worrying about everything that might go wrong.

Don't be afraid to fail. We already touched on this one briefly, but a lot of people never develop their gut instincts because they are terrified of failure, and in order to avoid failing, they overanalyze everything, always looking for data to back up their decisions. If you can let go of this fear of failure and trust your gut, you'll actually be on your way to better developing your intuition for the future. The only way to develop your gut instinct is by leaning into it—a scary experience sometimes, but also exciting, and something that will lead you into a new life!

Trust God. I don't know if there's a better way to develop your intuition than this one. When we talk about gut feelings in the Christian worldview, we're adding a whole new dimension to the idea of intuition, because if you believe in God and you believe the Holy Spirit is with you and influencing you, then you have access to an entirely new plane of understanding and knowledge. A Christian isn't just relying on their gut; they're also relying on God to give them wisdom and understanding, often in the moment. Many of the times when I'm trusting my gut, my intuition, my instincts—whatever you want to call it—I'm saying a prayer at the same time, asking God to lead me in the right direction.

Trust yourself. As we saw in the Kevin O'Leary quote, only you have your experience, only you have seen what you have seen, only you have lived what you have lived. When the stakes are high, can you trust that your experiences will lead you in the right direction? Of course, it's always important to seek out the wise counsel of other people—after all, they have different experiences and may have a different gut reaction—but it's always important to remember that they are not you. They don't have your instincts. So even if something seems cut-and-dried to someone else, a no-brainer decision, don't overlook that little voice inside you that's saying, "Hold off." If you're feeling conflicted about something that seems obvious to someone else, maybe it's your gut instinct making calculations based on your own experiences, and maybe it's something you need to listen to.

Kristin and I dated for a full four years before we got married—and most of the time was long-distance. It was no joke, and while dating her was fun, I could have done without the two thousand miles between us. Being apart from her every day was so tough. The time zone, even though it was only three hours, was the worst. I'd try to call her, but she was just waking up. Then she'd try to call me, but I was out doing stuff, and then I'd try to call her, but she was eating lunch, and then she'd try to call me, but I was eating dinner. The timing was always off, which made communication very difficult.

There were plenty of doubting voices in my ear at the time, questioning my reasoning for being locked in a long-distance relationship. It was during this time that I was living in the same apartment complex with the top twenty Viners in the world—my peers. It was an insane time in my life. Everyone there was always going to wild parties—it was the classic Hollywood story.

I remember going to a party down the hall in my complex. After the party began to fizzle out, a guy I knew invited me up to his apartment. It was on the top story, a corner unit, and I had always wanted to see what the inside of those looked like, so I followed him up.

Before I knew it, he had walked out to the balcony with his girlfriend, and another girl came into the room at the same time. She began to make small talk, but I didn't really pay any attention. In fact, I thought it was strange that he had invited me to his apartment to see it and then immediately went outside to the balcony and closed the door for what seemed to be a private romantic moment with his girlfriend. Eventually I walked over to the glass balcony door and stood there to get his attention.

He poked his head inside.

"Dude," he said, "that girl likes you."

I shrugged. "I have a girlfriend, man."

He laughed. "I know you always say that, but she lives, what, two thousand miles away? Is it that serious?"

"Yeah," I said, "it's that serious."

"Man, she really likes you," he said again, talking about the girl who had just left.

"Are you stupid?" I asked, laughing. "I said I have a girlfriend."

After more than a year of long distance, the honeymoon

feelings of dating Kristin for the first time had worn off, but I was still in love with her, and my intuition that we would get married kept me going through those long years apart.

When it comes to gut feelings, you just know. I wasn't conflicted at all, and having that steadfast kind of knowledge kept me on the right track. It was the same way with my documentary *Yard Boys*, the same way with Vine, the same way with the musical. I was unwavering. I knew what the next thing would be for me, and when I feel that way, no one can stop me. I'm going to do it, no matter who comes along and questions it.

Wedding days usually come and go so fast, like a blink, but mine felt kind of slow actually. I'm really grateful for that. To be able to live and linger in that moment and to remember my experience in full are huge blessings.

As great as the day was, it didn't start off quite so well. We were having an outdoor wedding, but it looked like rain was on the way, accompanied by a tornado warning. It was insane. And of course we had a backup plan—a pavilion where we could have the wedding if the weather got bad—but some of what we had planned wouldn't have worked well there. I was praying hard that it wouldn't rain.

Then the rain came, about forty-five minutes before the wedding was supposed to start. And it wasn't a Florida downpour; it was actually a really light rain that settled the dust, and then the sky completely cleared, and it wasn't muddy at all. The temperature dropped to a perfect 75 degrees.

It felt like God was watching over us. It was perfect.

We had a live band, which I think was one of the things that made the whole day so special. They were so good. And yes, hiring the band took us way over our budget, but both

Kristin and I didn't think we'd regret it—and we didn't. They were a full eight-piece band with horns and everything, and I even got to play with them, at one point going up on the stage and taking over the drums.

Everyone was dancing and joyful and smiling. You know how you go to some weddings and the DJ is practically begging people to come on out and dance, and everyone goes up for "Y.M.C.A," but that's it? Nothing like that at our wedding. Everyone was dancing, everyone on their feet from the beginning of the reception to the end. Everyone was jumping up and down to "Johnny B. Goode."

It was a great day.

In typical Marcus Johns fashion, I did rip my pants. I went down to do a little split move and tore them front to back. What can you do? I still have them in my closet.

Basically, everyone I know has told me that our wedding was the best wedding they've ever been to. I know a lot of people say that a lot of the time, but I just know that ours was legitimately one of the greats. The people we know from YouTube see the video, and even they can see there's something special—the video of that day exudes the fun and joy we had. It was awesome.

One of the main reasons that very special day took place was because I trusted my gut.

I went with my instinct. When I first met Kristin and we started dating, and when we were in the middle of what felt like a never-ending long-distance relationship, I trusted that my intuition—that I was going to marry this girl—was right.

What are you waiting for? Is there something in your life that your gut is telling you to do but you're not sure because there's no data, there's no physical evidence, backing up your gut? Is there a business you want to start or a person you want to ask out or something you want to create?

Trust your gut! Give it a shot. It's going to lead you to a new and exciting place.

CHAPTER 9

Imposter Syndrome

You would think that by chapter 9 I would feel good about this.

That I got the whole writing thing down by now.

That all doubts I previously had about my abilities to write a book have flown out the window.

But to be completely frank, chapter 8 took me three times as long as any chapter. I would write one sentence and then stop and think. *What am I doing? Is this even good enough? Who am I to be writing this book?*

I was just stuck and unmotivated.

Imposter syndrome can be one of the most crippling things one can go through in the creative process. When *you* don't even believe in yourself, who else could ever believe in you?

After finally finishing the musical, I remember having a deep sense of satisfaction that I had accomplished an extremely difficult feat. It's one of the huge rewards of the creative process, one of the amazing things about getting past the "You can't do it" voices.

It felt really good.

I had made a musical.

We had performed it in front of a sold-out house multiple times.

After each night, people would come up and ask . . .

"You wrote all of that music? That's unbelievable!"

"You put together that entire script? I didn't know you could do that!"

"You composed the score? Wow. Where'd you learn that?"

People were surprised because the musical was actually good.

But something about the tone of their voice communicated that they hadn't expected me to be able to create a musical, at least not one they would enjoy as much as they did.

In other words, they didn't think I had it in me. They were surprised.

And before I knew it, I was starting to feel kind of surprised too. Like, how *had* I done it? And I started undermining my own success.

I started to believe other people's—hmm, maybe we'll call it—*skepticism*. As more and more people came up to me and said, "Wow, I can't believe you did this," I started feeding off their energy and thinking, *Maybe I couldn't have done all of this. Could I? Did I?*

Had I really written a good musical?

Had everyone enjoyed it as much as they said they had?

And at the heart of it all was this question that the negative voices started whispering in my mind . . .

Did I just get lucky?

Imposter syndrome.

To be honest, I'd heard of the term before, but for a long time I didn't know exactly what it meant. Then I came across this definition:

> noun: anxiety or self-doubt that results from persistently undervaluing one's competence and active

> role in achieving success, while falsely attributing one's accomplishments to luck or other external forces.[14]

Oh, okay.

Self-doubt. Undervaluing my competence. Falsely thinking it was all just luck.

Imposter syndrome.

Yeah, I have that.

I have that hard-core.

And I think a lot of us have it, don't we? We create something that people enjoy, but instead of soaking up the encouragement and the good reviews, we start looking around skeptically, feeling kind of suspicious of the praise, and we start to doubt ourselves.

But why? Why are so many of us creative people walking around with all this self-doubt from continuously undervaluing our experience and know-how? Why do we keep saying, when someone compliments the work we've done, that we just got lucky?

Right place right time, I guess.

I had the right connections.

It wasn't THAT great.

We sometimes use these responses to explain away our talent and hard work and falsely file away some of our greatest achievements as luck.

Where Imposter Syndrome Comes From

If you start reading about super successful people in any field, but especially in creative areas like acting, writing, or music, you'll discover that most of those people reached a point early on in their careers where they felt like they were faking it, like all of their success was coming because of luck or some crazy, cosmic oversight.

So what is it about success that makes so many of us creative people doubt ourselves? Here are three things that may be causing imposter syndrome:

1. Comparison. I think one of the main reasons a lot of us deal with imposter syndrome is that we're obsessed with measuring ourselves against the knowledge and performance of others. Imposter syndrome is born out of comparison. We hold ourselves up to other people who have succeeded, and we don't think we could ever be as good as them or as beautiful as them or as talented as them.

Then when we do have success, we explain it away.

I must have gotten lucky.

The timing was right.

It all happened because I knew the right people.

A lot of times this happens if we're just starting out and consider ourselves amateurs in a new field. Others around us have been doing it for a lot longer than we have, so we undervalue our results, thinking something out of the ordinary must have happened for us to be so successful.

Or maybe we're not formally educated in a certain field, and we compare ourselves to those who have studied for years and years. When we have more success than the formally educated experts, we downplay what we've accomplished.

Of course, every situation is different and every person is different, and there's really no benefit in comparing ourselves to others and their levels of success. I'm me. You're you. Every journey is different.

2. False humility. Another reason some of us get all tangled up in imposter syndrome, especially as Christians, is that we've been taught to be humble. Some of the subtle (or not so subtle) messages you may have received through the years sound a lot like this:

Don't make a big deal about yourself.

Don't promote yourself or the work you're doing.

If you celebrate your success, you're just being prideful.

Real Christians downplay their accomplishments.

The thing is, God created you to do things that only you can do. When you have success, it's worth getting excited about! False humility—pretending you're not as good at something as you really are, or downplaying the things you love to do—isn't helping anyone.

3. Being unsure of how it all happened. This one happens a lot, and it's probably one of the biggest causes of imposter syndrome. You tried something new. You pulled it off. It was a huge success.

And honestly? You're not even completely sure how it happened.

Why it went so well.

Or even if you could replicate it.

There's a certain amount of pressure that starts to build up inside us when others say, "You're so good!" but we don't know how we pulled it off and we're pretty sure we'll never be able to do it again. Our success can sometimes create a new level, a higher expectation, and we start to lose sleep while wondering how we will ever live up to that version of ourselves again.

Sometimes when we're surprised by our own success, our own greatness, we resort to imposter syndrome to explain it all away. Don't forget all of the work you put into getting to that point. It didn't happen by accident.

Overcoming Imposter Syndrome

I felt all of those things when I finished the musical.

I started comparing *Viral* to other musicals, started comparing my lyrics to the lyrics of stuff on Broadway, started comparing my way of doing things to the way other shows did things.

I felt a false humility settling in on all of my conversations, as if I had to convince people that I knew I wasn't that great, that I understood I was new to the game. That for what it was, it was pretty good.

It really started to hit me that if I talked to any real pros in the business, they would figure out so fast how rudimentary everything about the musical was. They'd learn that I can't even read music, and that if I had to play all the songs on the piano right now, I probably couldn't even do it. I started to focus on all of the holes in my musical, hoping they wouldn't expose me for the fraud that I was.

Imposter syndrome began to completely take over. But with time, I worked my way through it and found the confidence in myself and in my show.

Here's how.

Keep putting in the work. You have to realize that there is no mental shortcut or phrase you can say or tell yourself that will jumpstart the confidence you need to overcome imposter syndrome. It's just not as simple as saying certain words or phrases and suddenly realizing you had your mojo all along. The main thing you have to do in order to ditch the anxiety or self-doubt is to continually put in the work. Anyone will get rusty if you break from something long enough.

You have to get back into the work.

The good part is, everything is easier the second time around, and the third time, and then the fourth time. You'll be surprised at how quickly you improve when you commit to the work, and when you do, it will give you the confidence you need. It's like riding a bike—everything is like riding a bike! You just have to be willing to get back on. Sometimes that means breaking out the training wheels for a time. There's no shame in that.

Reengage previous talents and knowledge. If you ask me right now if I can play the guitar, I'll say no. Well, actually, I can play one song. Maybe three or four chords. Except that's not true—in reality, I know a ton of chords and can play a lot of songs. I can play the guitar, but out of this kind of false humility, I'll say, "No, I can't play the guitar."

After months of producing other aspects of the show, I didn't play the music myself for months. A few weeks after our performances, I began to go into rewrites and felt so disconnected from the music. *How do I play this again?* I would think of all the people saying, "Wow, and you composed the music too?" and it made me feel like a fraud. I literally had to rediscover how I performed those songs. I went back to the original recording files I had made, got the basic chords, and plunked away. Day after day, it slowly began to come back to me. Two weeks later, I believed myself again when I said, "Yes, yes I did."

Sometimes reengaging with your previous talents and knowledge will remind you how much you know and how good you really are.

Reject artificial humility. As I mentioned before, imposter syndrome can often ignite an artificial humility in us, and sometimes artificial humility can actually get in the way of us being truly humble. How often have you said you can't do something when in fact you can? How often have you downplayed your talents because you "don't want to brag"?

When you speak words, they become life, so be careful—if you keep saying you're not good at something, you might start to believe yourself. If you keep downplaying your ability, you might just throw yourself off track.

Own it—you *are* a fraud. Wait? But I thought you just said . . .

Hear me out. I often think if people knew how little I know about music or music theory, they would think I was a fraud. Right? So the fact is, I don't know anything about music theory. Not one single, solitary thing. When I write music, I come up with the melody in my head and then plink it out on the piano, one solitary note at a time. Then I play a root note for a chord and painstakingly figure out the chord I'm trying to play in my head. Over and over.

Plink.

Plink.

Plink.

Oh, that sounds good. Let's go with that.

So instead of pretending that I know anything about music theory, instead of fighting with this imposter syndrome thing in my head where it keeps telling me I'm a fraud, I'll just say it out loud.

I am a fraud.

I am not the musician you might think I am.

Instead of trying to pretend I'm an expert, instead of trying to put up a good front that convinces everyone I am something I'm not, I find it helpful to just put it out there.

I'm not formally trained.

I never studied music in school.

I don't know anything about music theory.

When you wear your shortcomings like a badge of honor,

the fear of being exposed will have no power over you. And imposter syndrome will begin to melt away.

Now, when owning that you're a fraud, don't go too far. For example, I would be practicing artificial humility if I said, "I'm not a composer," or "I'm not a writer." Because I am both of those things. But I don't want to get into this whole *Wizard of Oz* thing, where I'm creating a facade of being a huge, scary, green guy when I'm actually just a man hiding behind a curtain pushing random buttons.

Know that imposter syndrome, in small doses, isn't a bad thing. To some degree, I think imposter syndrome can be healthy if you don't let it control you. It can be good to have a healthy fear of the task at hand, especially if that fear motivates you to work harder and learn more and improve. The opposite of having imposter syndrome is talking a big game and then not being able to back it up.

Imposter syndrome can even be a gift. Because while it might drive the average person to hide or give up, it might actually encourage you to do something completely different—imposter syndrome might motivate you to learn more about the field you're in, and it might push you to find out what's actually behind your success.

Maybe when you start to push against imposter syndrome, you'll learn the formula that led to your success.

The feeling of imposter syndrome has driven me to want to learn more about music. After finishing the musical, I've recognized there is an infinite amount I don't understand, and I'd like to fill in some of those gaps, not to impress people, but so I can get better at what I do.

In this way, imposter syndrome has driven me to a certain degree.

Let it drive you.

The Opposite of Imposter Syndrome . . .

. . . is know-it-all syndrome.

You don't want to be the know-it-all.

Trust me.

Experts are people who have already studied it all. And those people, the ones who have all the theory and the knowledge in the world, are usually tempted to hold themselves, and the stuff they create, to an impossible standard. They've studied it all, including the masterpieces and the experts, the classics and the critics' favorites, and if the expert can't create something that will fit in among the all-time greats in their field, they won't even start.

They're paralyzed, because they know they can't live up to the greats.

They're stuck, because they don't know what to make that could possibly be as good as Shakespeare or Mozart or Monet.

They see everything besides the classics as rudimentary, and this includes their own efforts, so they quit before they ever begin.

You'll never satisfy that kind of mind-set, because that way of seeing things, that über-expert way of looking at life, requires you to get deeper and deeper, more and more obscure.

It makes me think about these silly little gas bikes I'm building. At first, I would tell people about what I was working on, and 90 percent of people were like, "What? I've never even heard of that!" And they were amazed. They thought it was so cool.

But now that I've gone a little further in the process and have visited online forums, I have to admit I would be slightly embarrassed to put up a how-to video on YouTube, because there are guys out there who are experts at this, who modify every little thing on their bikes, and who know way more than I do. I'm learning that you can put on certain exhaust pipes in order to go faster, and if you add this particular sprocket or upgrade your ignition coil . . .

blah blah blah . . .

Wait.

Listen.

What I'm about to tell you is super important.

There is always going to be someone who is way smarter than you.

Did you hear that?

I'll say it again for those of you in the back.

There is always going to be someone who is way smarter than you.

There is always going to be an expert who knows more than you do about that thing you love to do.

Once you've built that first bike, you'll want to go faster. You'll want more information. You'll find more experts. And that's okay, but just remember two things:

1. You don't have to be an expert to enjoy what you're doing.
2. About 90 percent of people will think it's cool you built a bike.

Most people will love the stuff you put out, even if you're not an expert.

Especially if you're not an expert.

Being an imposter (and by imposter, I mean someone who is doing more than others may think you're qualified to do) totally beats the alternative of knowing everything and never doing anything with it.

There are experts in music theory who will never write a musical because they're paralyzed at the thought of writing something average.

There are experts in art theory who will never paint anything because they don't think they can measure up against the greats.

There are experts in your field who are too scared to actually do anything.

You *are* an imposter. You're operating outside of your expertise. You're trying to do things others don't think you're qualified to do. You're stretching yourself.

Those are not bad things.

Those are really good things.

Don't be afraid to be seen as an imposter, as someone who is doing more than you're qualified to do. Just own it, and keep going.

CHAPTER 10

There Is Work to Be Done

In October 2019, I released a video called "How Much Money Can You Make from a Gumball Machine?"

I know.

It sounds kind of ridiculous.

Basically, three of my friends and I decided we were all going to buy a gumball machine and see who could make the most money. We could buy whichever gumball machine we wanted, and we could put whatever candy into the machine that we chose.

The prize?

Whoever made the most money in a month won all of the profits from all of the machines.

Pretty simple, right?

Of course, we couldn't just go out and buy brand-new gumball machines at Walmart or wherever you find that kind of thing. I decided we'd first visit a junkyard of gumball machines.

Besides, it would save us some money.

We arrived at the house of a man who had hundreds of gumball machines stacked in his two-car garage and around his house. We negotiated with him for a while and ended up getting our machines for forty bucks each.

So off we went, the four of us, each with our own

machine, to find a place to put them and see who could make the most money.

When I asked Kristin what she thought about my new gumball millionaire plan, her response proved how well she knows me.

"I have a feeling you're going to get in way too deep."

Yep.

I filled my machine and tried to find a place to put it, and my first spot ended up being in a thrift store. They wanted to do a 30/70 split. It wasn't ideal for the competition, but I didn't feel bad about giving them 30 percent because it was a charity.

Then we went with my brother, Cody, as he pitched to some different locations. He didn't have a lot of luck, but eventually he ended up placing his in a nail salon.

My friend Jon landed a spot for his machine, Priscilla's Coffee Shop in Burbank, right next to the Warner Bros. lot. Which was great until one of their employees said they were allergic to nuts. And he had filled his machine with peanut M&Ms. So. We had to switch his to actual gumballs.

Finally, Andy found a spot for his machine inside a small café.

After thirty days, we went back to check the machines.

Here's the thing about the gumball machine challenge—it's inherently silly, right? And there was this safety net, knowing I was doing it as a YouTube video, with no strings attached, no expectations.

But here's the other thing about the gumball machine challenge—I go into everything I do thinking, *Hey, this could be the big one. This could be the video that takes off. This could be the business idea that really works.* I never phone in any of my ideas. In this case, we really did believe it could be the beginning of a small gumball empire. It's probably what makes the video so entertaining—all of us guys actually care so much about these machines and how well they do. We raised the stakes so high for something that is not so high stakes.

That's how I always am. It's just the way my brain is wired. I honestly believe that anything I choose to do could go big.

So why in the heck am I telling you about a gumball machine video during which I made a few bucks selling candy in a month?

For me, it all comes back to a quote by P. T. Barnum, the founder of Barnum & Bailey's Greatest Show on Earth.

"Fortune always favors the brave, and never helps a man who doesn't help himself."[15]

I love that quote, and there have been variations of it through the years, but they all circle back around to the idea that you have to keep moving. Don't worry about being perfect.

Gary Vaynerchuk is a super famous author and entrepreneur, and before he was as crazy famous as he is now, I got to hang out with him a bit in the early days of Vine. We went to his office on many occasions during that time because his was the first company doing sponsored posts with creators on Vine. I remember him forecasting how Vine would disappear in a few years. None of us believed him until it happened. Even when he was saying crazy prophetic things like that, I always thought he was such a smart guy. In his book *Crushing It!* he taps into a P. T. Barnum–type vein when he writes:

> Being unafraid of making mistakes makes everything easy for me. Not worrying about what people

> think frees you to do things, and doing things allows you to win or learn from your loss—which means you win either way. Hear me now: you are better off being wrong ten times and being right three than you are if you try only three times and always get it right.[16]

I love that. If I keep moving, keep trying, even keep failing, with speed, I'm eventually going to have way more success than someone who weighs up every opportunity meticulously and is afraid to start. It's better to be three out of thirteen than three for three, because in the first instance I've learned so much more than the person who is three for three.

You have to be bold.

You have to be willing to make mistakes.

You have to be willing to work harder than anyone else.

It's easy to get caught up in trying not to make mistakes. We don't want people to see us flop, right? We don't want these things on our record (and with the internet, this stuff is *always* on our record) for others to see in the future. So in order to make sure everything is a home run, we only try one or two ventures.

Not me.

I want to have it on my record.

I want to have a few flops.

When I've got flops in my history, it means I'm that much closer to hitting it big.

Fortune favors the bold.

It's true. You have to be bold about it. Right now, Cody and I are pitching a new show, and it's just another idea. We're endless-idea guys. I'm going to have a million ideas, and all that has to stick is one of them.

It reminds me of my dad's quote: "I can come up with ten bad ideas before you can come up with one good one."

You can't be afraid of bad ideas. I might have bad ideas, but I'm not afraid to say them out loud. Or try them.

If the idea doesn't pay off, then by all means, move on! But you can't be afraid to try.

The Chicken Coop

I've got another story about how the hardest worker wins, and it doesn't have anything to do with gumball machines (which I'll get back to in a minute). But it is just as obscure.

First let me say, our family is made up of "idea people." We really think a lot about things, mull over ideas, and talk about some of the stupidest things in depth. I guess that's just how we are. We like to see everything from different angles.

This story tells of another time when my dad was in town and we wanted to build something.

But this time it wasn't a shed.

We weren't hanging light fixtures.

It didn't involve working on an engine (or putting out a car fire).

This time, my brother, Cody, wanted to build a chicken coop. Big deal, right? So, build yourself a chicken coop. Well, the problem was, he lived on a very steep hillside up in the Hills, and basically my dad, Cody, and I all had different ideas on the best way to build a chicken coop on a very steep hillside. I mean, it was like a seventy-degree incline. If you took a wrong step, you were going for a long tumble.

"We can't build it up here on the hill," my dad said. "We'll have to build it down at the bottom of the hill because that's where it's flat."

"Yeah, I don't know," Cody said. "I don't want to do that—it's a steep walk to get all the way down there."

"Guys," I interrupted, "look, this is the perfect place—right where we're standing."

We were standing in the middle of the steepest part of the hill under some trees.

"No way," my dad said. "You can't do that. It's way too steep. We'll have to think of something else."

"We can just dig it out," I said.

And they both replied, "There's no way."

So the two of them went inside to talk it out, weigh up the options. But I knew my spot was ideal.

Aside from the massively steep hill part.

But more importantly, I had heard the words, "There's no way." Those words are my own personal nemesis.

So I grabbed a shovel and started digging. I'm not the kind of person who worries about getting my hands dirty—it was in the middle of a 100-degree summer day, and I took off my shirt and dug like a madman. I dug as fast as I could, hoping they would talk for a while to buy me enough time to make the progress I needed in order to sell my vision. By the time they came back out, they realized it was too late, and that was the route we'd go, because 75 percent of it was done in forty-five minutes of nonstop shoveling. All they could do was take their turn with the shovel and dig.

My dad loves that old saying, "How do you eat an elephant? One bite at a time," and even though it's a common expression, I love it too. Sometimes, most of the time, you just have to get started by doing the little bit you know how to do.

It took us about an hour and a half, and there it was—a

nice flat spot for the chicken coop. I even dug out a little walkway to it.

So whose idea won? The best idea? The cheapest idea? Nah. It was the person who took charge and blazed the trail.

Those are the ideas that usually win.

What Hard Work Will Do to You

There's just something about hard work that solves a lot of the problems we face as creative people. I know I've mentioned this in some of the previous chapters—hard work is crucial to attaining success.

So, what is it about hard work that brings about success?

Here are five things that happen when you work hard:

1. When you work hard on something you love, you become obsessed with it (in a good way). I don't think I ever worked harder than I did during the Vine years. I put in more work and spent more hours on Vine than anyone else.

Period.

When I first started, my initial goal was to get to a thousand followers.

One thousand.

The only way I knew to get followers was a pretty straightforward strategy: I spent eighteen hours a day on my phone on Vine. I would sleep for five or six hours and then get up and go back to work. I landed almost all of those thousand followers by literally liking and commenting on about ten thousand posts. I scrolled through, watched a random person's video under the hashtag #firstvine, and commented something specific to their video so they knew I had actually watched it and wasn't just a spammer who was saying, "Hey, follow me!" With that strategy, I was able to convert one in ten of those people into followers. That was a pretty good return, especially in the early days, and that's how I built my initial tiny base.

I spent all of my time doing that. I was obsessed.

I think I got to my initial goal of one thousand followers by the end of the first week. It was just me doing the thing I loved, putting in the hours, and doing the work. Along with posting multiple videos a day, of course.

From there I went from zero to one million followers in three months.

This all happened before the internet had evolved in a way to help things go viral. There weren't all of those things in place to shoot you to the top—you had to fight and claw for every like, every share, every follower. The system was much, much different back then.

But I hit my goals for one reason: I simply outworked everyone else.

2. When you work hard, you create new relationships. As things got even busier on my Vine account, thousands of comments began pouring in on my videos, with lots of people loving what I was doing (for the most part) and encouraging me. So, what did I do with those comments? Did I sit back and enjoy my newfound celebrity status? Did I kick up my feet and drift peacefully into the future?

Ha! No, I kept working hard.

In fact, this may sound kind of crazy, but I tried to reply to every comment during the first year because I knew these were the people who would help me grow. Every comment. I can't say I actually did reply to every single one, but that was my goal.

I wanted every person who watched one of my videos

to become a true fan—not just an observer, but an active participant in the creative life of Marcus Johns.

They weren't simply sending the video link on the platform to their friends, "Oh, check out this video." (You couldn't even do that in the early days.) No, they were telling everyone they knew, "Look at this Marcus Johns video! I commented, and he actually replied. How crazy is that? I really like this guy. Oh, wait, watch this one too."

That was the response I was going for.

I wanted to create as many real relationships, as many genuine interactions, as possible. I wanted to exude a certain kind of friendly personality, an aura of friendship. I started seeing the same people commenting, and we'd end up having small conversations in the comments section of my videos.

If you look at popular videos now, most creators aren't even responding to anyone.

Not one single reply.

But I commented back to everyone.

And on top of that, I would meet fans in person in cities all across America for free, and I was the first on Vine to do this. Reaching out of the screen and into my fans' personal lives was something I just wanted to do naturally, and it ended up being worthwhile in the long run.

Creating these personal relationships with fans was a big reason why I grew so fast.

3. Working hard involves repetition, which leads to mastery. The hard work of creating an actual Vine video may not sound like very much. After all, we're talking a six-second video, right? How much work can you actually put into creating a six-second video?

A lot.

I probably averaged thirty takes for every Vine. Sometimes I'd do more than a hundred takes. Sometimes I'd get it right on the first try.

It seems to me that most of the time I either nailed it on the first or second take, or it took dozens of attempts to get it just right. In either case, I was aiming for a video that looked like it was off-the-cuff, natural. That's why the first-take Vines were always the best. Something about them just felt like I was capturing lightning in a bottle. I was always chasing that first-take quality.

I couldn't get that natural first-take vibe every day, so I would have to put in the time and go take after take after take. I had the person or the props or the time only to pull off that Vine for that day. Even though it wasn't going to be easy, I felt I had to do it.

Because I worked so hard, because I spent so much time on the platform, and because I did things over and over and over again, I got to a certain level of mastery within the Vine system and was able to capture the quality much more quickly as time passed.

I soon learned which types of videos were going to work on the first or second take and what would require a hundred takes—and soon I could even recognize that before I started.

You're not going to get good at what you love to do by wasting time and procrastinating. You can have success—you can do it!—but if you want to be the best, you have to work harder than anyone else. With repetition comes mastery.

No one accidentally gets to the top.

4. Working hard closes the gap between really good and great.

Listen, let's be honest, everyone is okay with 95 percent effort. If you get a 95 percent in a class you're taking, no one is going to be upset by that. It's a good grade. If you put in 95 percent effort at work or at school, you're going to get solid results.

Seriously.

95 percent is not bad.

People will like you.

But you won't be the best.

The difference between 95 percent and 98 percent is the difference between really good and great. But to get from 95 percent to 98 percent doesn't require 3 percent more work; it requires 500 percent more work.

Think about it this way. It's a lot like running. If you can sprint 100 yards in twenty seconds, your journey to fifteen seconds is totally doable. You can probably even do it relatively quickly by focusing on your start and finish alone. Just about anyone can shave 25 percent off their initial time if they're consistent and have the right approach.

But getting from fifteen seconds to ten seconds is going to be tough! And to get from ten seconds to nine seconds is monumental! Because the closer you get to perfection, the harder it is to improve. As sprinters get faster and faster, it becomes almost impossible for them to improve by one-tenth of a second.

At Vine, I wanted to close the gap between me and perfection. I wanted to really understand how Vine worked, how the algorithm was designed, how I could maximize my potential. Getting my videos on the popular page (where they listed the videos that were trending with the most views per second) became a game to me. I watched how other people posted, when other people posted, how they titled their videos, exactly how long the videos were, and how they interacted on the other social media platforms.

I was so obsessed with having the number one spot and being top dog that I created my own algorithm for optimal posting. I remember that posting at exactly 3:29 p.m. East Coast time was the best time to post my videos on Vine—that's when all the kids were coming out of school, and back then they weren't allowed to have phones on in school, so they'd all turn their phones on and check Vine. They would refresh the feed every seven minutes on the popular page, so posting at 3:29 would allow me to generate the most amount of likes in that seven-minute period, ranking me higher. I had this time figured out perfectly.

And it worked. All of those tiny details, going above and beyond, is what closed the gap between good and great for me.

5. Working hard helps you to follow your passion. Hard work has a great way of clarifying for you what you actually love to do and what you can let go of. If you work really, really hard at something, you're going to get sick of it pretty fast unless you love it.

Vine was kind of a random passion for me, something I latched on to. I mean, I love to act, and I love to make videos, and I love to entertain, but there were a lot of directions I could have gone with that. Vine just so happened to be the perfect storm, bringing all my interests together.

The thing is, I knew I loved doing it because I was spending all that time on it and didn't make a dime, not at first. And at the time, there wasn't anyone who had made any serious money from making videos on the internet.

Thank goodness I was a college student who had all kinds of time, because Vine has become the thing that sustained me financially for the last seven or eight years. It led me into so many of the things I do now, and it bought me the time I needed to do other things I loved, like making a musical, writing a book, and having a YouTube audience. Vine gave me a fan base, followers, and the money I needed to keep following my dreams, big and small.

Hard work will help steer you in this direction because it will help you figure out what you love to do and what you don't love to do.

When Life (and Love) Collides with Your Work Habits

Here's something you may not have thought about.

You can be cruising along, working super hard, making progress, closing the gap between 95 percent and 98 percent, and then . . .

WHAM!

Life circumstances can bring about some quick changes.

Getting married was a huge shift in my work life.

Getting married to Kristin was hands down the best decision I've ever made in my life. It also brought about some serious changes, mostly because I suddenly had to learn how to live with someone else all the time.

Getting married rocked my world.

For the first three months after we were married, I began to realize that Kristin didn't like going to bed by herself at night, which meant I couldn't stay up until 3:00 a.m. . . . which is when I'm most productive and creative, the time I usually work on my writing and editing. Some people are morning people. Some are night people. But what happens when your significant other is on the opposite schedule from you?

The long distance between us while we were dating put our relationship out of sync, but then we got married and were more out of sync than I thought we'd be. Adjusting from my usual LA lifestyle and workflow into my new married life was definitely a culture shock.

My videomaking process mostly relied on me getting hit with inspiration, calling up a few friends, taking over the house for the day, filming, eating, hanging out, and then . . . staying up all night editing. Except after I got married, I realized I needed to call Kristin first to make sure she didn't have plans at home that day or needed to film her own stuff. And maybe it might get weird because she doesn't vibe with this guy I'm going to work with. There were so many things to arrange, to check on, to make sure Kristin was okay with.

I realized I wasn't a bachelor anymore.

I realized I had to schedule out my work ahead of time.

I realized I had to put someone else first.

I never had to do that before. I never had to say to myself, *I wonder what this other person thinks about my plans for the day.* This new lifestyle wasn't exactly conducive to my sort of off-the-wall, scatterbrained style of filming. So when we first got married, I withdrew from my work a little bit because I felt like I couldn't be productive in my usual manner.

I decided to take a step back and help support Kristin because she was really starting to take off with her own YouTube channel. I wanted to help her build her own brand, and I knew that part of achieving that meant I had to mature out of being the "sometimes I just don't care" guy. The crazy guy. I had to figure out how to be a family man.

In some ways, the idea came before the man.

I had to start acting like the person I knew I had to

become. The “a little more responsible” husband who still liked to do his zany projects but also did laundry . . . sometimes.

Who am I kidding? I don’t do the laundry.

But I do the dishes. That’s our deal. Dishes and trash. Hey! Dishes was a big step for me, because before Kristin, I ate out every single meal for five years.

Anyway. You get the point.

But now I’m having fun with my creativity again and doing what I want on my usual creative schedule. Now that we’ve been married for a few years, there’s more flexibility than there was in the honeymoon stage. We’ve gotten used to seeing each other a lot, and our relationship has developed to the point where we’re giving each other a little more independence again, because, *Hey, I’ll see ya tomorrow too, ya know.*

Relationships are hard work. It was work during the long-distance phase of life, and it was hard work when we were finally together all the time as newlyweds. But the work has paid off, because now I have a life partner and my days are ten times better in every way than they were before I was married. Efficiency, income, lifestyle . . . it’s all better.

But it took a season of very hard work, and in some ways the hard work of marriage will never vanish. But it’s changed now in ways that free me up to return to my creative endeavors.

It reminds me of these hedges I planted at my house. When I first planted them, I had to water them by hand every single day to make sure they were getting enough moisture and the roots were taking in the ground. It was, quite frankly, not always the thing I wanted to do.

But now?

The roots are so deep I don't have to water them at all! Not even if we go a few weeks without rain. They grow on their own because of the hard work I put in at the beginning when they were little baby plants.

That's how hard work is—it's an investment in whatever the thing is that you're working on.

Work hard on your marriage? It's an investment in that relationship.

Work hard where you're employed? It's an investment in that career.

Work hard on the thing you love to do? It's an investment in yourself and your future.

Hedges won't grow overnight. But once you put in the hard, early work, they can take off on their own.

Find the Road Less Traveled

When we showed up at the thrift store to pick up the money from my gumball machine, you can imagine my disappointment when I saw a handful of quarters in the tank. Then as we started walking away with the machine, a very determined employee came outside and nearly performed a citizen's arrest on me because she thought I was stealing it!

To be fair, it did have a sticker on it labeling it as property of the thrift store, but we had only put it on the machine so customers wouldn't think it was for sale.

When she threatened to call the police, I backed down. We all went into the back room, and I pleaded my case.

Kristin's words echoed in my mind: "I have a feeling Marcus is going to get in way too deep."

I felt like I was about to get arrested over this gumball machine.

Eventually, cooler heads prevailed, and we convinced them I did own the machine.

Mine wasn't the only strange experience. There was definitely some dodgy stuff going on with Cody's machine—we showed up and noticed that his M&M supply had gone way down, but there was only $2.75 in the tank. Either someone had been stealing his money or someone had been stealing his candy—or something else crazy had happened.

Once we added it all up, our friend Andy was the winner.

But the whole time, when you watch the video, you'll see how serious we all took it.

A lot of people would just be like, "Eh, what's the big deal? It's a gumball machine."

But I'm passionate about everything I do, so even though someone might think it's "stupid," I'm still taking it seriously.

Maybe that's why Kristin warned everyone she had a feeling I was going to get in too deep.

But that's a perfect description of me.

I get in deep.

And if something fails? Oh well. I did my best. I learned what I could learn. And then I move on.

I mean, that's the thing.

When people say, "Hey, wait a second, you can't do that . . . can you?" or they ask, "Is that even possible, or worth it?" I love it. When I'm getting questions like that, I know I'm in the right place at the right time, trying the right thing.

That's what gets me the most excited.

Because that means I'm on the road less traveled.

And those are always the most rewarding roads.

Speaking of roads, I love to drive my truck off-road, and so I'm always noticing the road that has all the signs—"No Trespassing" or "Restricted Access" or whatever. Blah blah blah. That's going to stop like 99 percent of people, and they're never going to ask about it or probably even think about it again. They see a restricted road, and they're movin' on.

Not me.

When I see a road like that, you know what I'm going to do?

First, I'm going to start asking a ton of questions.

Oh, that road's restricted?

I wonder why?

Actually, I wonder who owns that road?

And then I'm going to do the work. I'm going to head over to the LA County parcel office, do my research, find the mailing address, send them a real-life letter, and ask them if I can meet them because I've always been interested in that particular road or property.

I do this all the time.

Normally, I'll get a polite letter back or some message that thanks me for asking, but it's owned by such and such oil company or so and so power company. Whatever.

But sometimes, the road is owned by an individual.

And I'm going to put in the work to figure out how to access that road, because no matter what the signs say, there's always a way to get to where you want to go.

Always.

Anything is possible in this world.

The best things in life are found on the roads less traveled. Whenever you're hearing people say, "You can't do that!" it means you're at the right place. You're on the edge of starting down a less traveled road.

This is where the opportunities are.

This is where your new life begins.

Be ready to put in the work.

CHAPTER 11

Encouragement

It was the fall of 2019, and we had two months to find the perfect New York City theater for the showcase of *Viral*. A showcase is basically when you do a reading of the musical in front of a small group of potential investors and producers, people who have the clout to get a musical onto Broadway (or even off-Broadway).

It was our one shot.

So, you know. No pressure.

I flew into NYC from Los Angeles, had meetings, made some great connections (which I'll tell you about later), and generally got overwhelmed by that feeling of smallness most of us get when we're walking around a city of nine million people squeezed into one small space. I felt lost there among all the skyscrapers and the crowds and the lights.

It was actually kind of a nice feeling. Humbling in the best way.

So, anyway, in the midst of this crazy schedule, one of the more important items on the to-do list was to find a place to host the event, some kind of small theater that would really go well with what we were trying to do with *Viral*. Two of us spent an entire afternoon cruising the city, checking out potential venues.

The first place we went to was very bougie and had bad art everywhere and graffiti on the walls. It was supposed to be this cool, hip spot, but I just wasn't vibing with it. The only feeling it gave me was tacky. I have to admit, I was discouraged. This was one of the best available places, and we had pretty much banked on this being the spot we'd choose.

We tried another one too, but it just wasn't right. I had a vision for where *Viral* would be performed, and I knew the style of the theater would be super important. But there aren't a lot of affordable options in New York, and I knew this—and I also knew I might have to be flexible. We only had two months, after all. The date was right there, staring me down.

But there was one other place, a theater we had heard about from one of the companies we met with back in LA. They had only mentioned it in passing, but the name had stuck in my head, and it turned out we weren't too far from it.

"Let's just stop by," I said. "We can see if they rent out space. Couldn't hurt to ask, right?"

When we first walked up to it, I kind of wondered if it was a mistake. After opening the door, we were hit with a daunting set of industrial stairs with chipped-off white paint. It was a four-story staircase going straight up, no turns, just saying to us, "Climb me. I dare you." I thought to myself, *This is already a bad sign. Who is going to open the door, see these stairs, and be in a good mood to see a musical?* But then an older woman started hiking down the stairs, so I thought, *If she can do it, I have no excuse.* We squeezed past the woman and made it to the box office at the top of the stairs. We tapped on the glass to get the attention of the man sitting behind a desk so I could see if I could learn anything about the theater.

"Hey," I said, "we're just stopping in to see if we could get some info on renting the theater—maybe go in and take a look at one of the stages?"

He didn't look all that interested in helping us.

"Well, Katherine just left one minute ago, and she won't be back for a while. She had some errands to run."

Dang. The woman on the stairs was the person I needed to talk to, and we just whizzed right by her.

"Do you know what time she might come back?" I asked.

He just looked back at his computer. "No."

Hospitality was clearly not his strong suit.

"Well, do you mind if we just pop our heads inside to look at the theater?" I asked. "We're trying to narrow down a few different options."

"No, you can't do that," he said, and the look he gave me was obviously meant to say, *Anything else, chump?*

We wandered around a bit and then stood outside the theater for about fifteen minutes. I turned to Lily, our general manager on the show.

"Lil, what are we gonna do? Both the other places were bumped, and this is the only other theater that would remotely be in our price range."

We weighed the option of sneaking in, since Google maps showed some other entrances (turns out we entered the back way first). Maybe we could circumvent that guy at the box office and meet a janitor who could show us inside real quick.

We decide to try the front doors, even though we were pretty sure it would just lead us back to the same guy in the box office. When we got to the elevator, I had second thoughts.

"Wait," I said. I was disappointed and frustrated. "Let's

not even go up. This for sure is going to lead us right back to that annoying dude again."

We went back outside, talked for a little while longer, and made arrangements to go back to Brooklyn, where I was staying. I called my friend to let him know I was leaving the city to head back to his place and lined up my Uber. But just as I reserved it, the woman from the stairs walked up to the door. Lily and I quickly flagged her down and told her we had just missed her a few minutes before and how we wanted to see inside. To be honest, we were expecting to get shut down immediately, considering our first interaction, but it turned out she was the nicest woman in the entire world.

"Oh, come in!" she said. "You're here at the perfect time. We can help you out with whatever you need."

She took us right in and showed us around. The theater was perfect, exactly what I was looking for.

"I'm the general manager," she said matter-of-factly. "See all these seats? I bought them all for five dollars each when we first opened this place. And I carried them in here one by one with two Honduran guys."

She went on and on about the history of the theatre, and we found out she has the world record for most consecutive appearances in an off-Broadway play—more than thirteen thousand shows!

"Tell me about your musical," she said. So I told her about *Viral*. She asked about me and my interests, and I told her how I had gotten to where I was.

"Oh, my gosh," she gushed. "You're famous!" And she smiled. She was so sweet.

"We're looking to do a showcase," I said, and her eyes lit up.

"What are you going to do for food?" she asked.

I started answering, but she couldn't contain her excitement and just jumped right in.

"You have to bring hors d'oeuvres. Definitely. But no little sandwiches—they're too messy. And you also want to make sure . . ."

And she went on. And on. She gave us so much wonderful advice, telling us everything she knew about the industry, the people who would probably be there, and what to expect. She was excited without being bossy, enthusiastic without trying to take over the whole thing. She seemed genuinely happy to help.

When we walked out of the theater, I couldn't believe it.

That was where I wanted to be. The energy was amazing, and that's what I was looking for.

It turns out that *Hamilton* uses an entire wing of that theater for their rehearsal space. Yet she was gushing over how I was famous? LOL. She was too humble. She could have started off by name-dropping Lin-Manuel Miranda and his production using her theater, but she didn't. It was nice to see someone who had so many things going on in the legit theater world be so encouraging to little old me and the musical I was trying to get off the ground.

What had just happened?

Giving and receiving encouragement is one of the most important parts of a creative person's life. I have been so impacted by people encouraging me, and I love giving really intentional encouragement to others—not to the point that it's embarrassing—but I love telling people they're great and that, yes, they can do it!

Most of us don't get enough encouragement these days. But my parents were a given in my life. They always encouraged me, no matter what.

I was talking to someone else, someone in their late twenties, whose dream was to be an actress someday. But her parents had decided long before that she was going to be a doctor. So anytime she said her dream was to be an actress, she was met with the same response.

"What? Stop it. That's ridiculous. That doesn't happen. Get real—you're going to school to be a doctor, and that's that. Being an actress is a pipe dream."

That's so sad to me! I hate hearing how kids' dreams are stunted, even at a young age, before they've even had a chance to be tested.

My own parents' response was so different.

"Of course," they'd say. "If you want to do it, do it. Give it a shot. Why not?"

My dad went so far with this approach that even if he knew I was going to fail, he wouldn't stand in my way (within reason).

I remember there was a time when I thought I could put an electric trolling motor on a kayak and water-ski behind it. The thing is, we weren't allowed to use gas motors on the lake where I grew up, but we could use electric ones, so I figured if I put an electric motor on the back of a kayak and if someone paddled a little bit to help, I could get up on skis behind the kayak.

"Yeah, that's never going to work," my dad said. "There's not enough thrust. But, hey, give it a shot. Why not?"

That might not sound very encouraging, but the thing is, he was the guy who got in the kayak and paddled while operating the motor just because I wanted to see if it could be done. My dad was always willing to let me have dumb ideas and give them a try. I mean, if he thought I was going to hurt myself, he'd step in (most of the time), but other than that, he shrugged and said, "Go for it."

When I told him I wanted to be full-time Viner, he just said, "Go with your gut, Marcus. When you follow your passions, things usually turn out well."

Because I grew up with such encouraging parents, I always believed I could do anything. And when I made mistakes, I wasn't devastated, because I figured I'd just try it again.

They let me make mistakes.

They allowed me to try my dumb ideas.

And no, I couldn't get up on water skis behind a kayak with an electric engine.

My dad was right.

But I sure had fun trying.

Such small encouragements can lead to such big things.

Where would I be if my friend CJ hadn't encouraged me in my singing that long-ago day? Would I have tried out for the talent show? Would I have auditioned for the school's lead musical role?

It probably seemed like such a small thing to him at the time—those few minutes of praise and encouragement—but it literally changed my life.

Literally.

I don't even know if I would be doing this right now, if I would have written a musical.

It's the seemingly little things that keep you going for one more day.

And I wouldn't have been in that position to play and sing that song if it hadn't been for my brother Cody's encouragement. He has always encouraged me to try the things I want to do. He was a huge factor in my move to LA. He's the one who first taught me how to play the piano. He showed me how to play a Michael Bublé song, and I practiced it over and over and over again. Every day for a few days, he showed me all the chords, and I kept trying, even though it was difficult—I had no idea how to move my fingers over the piano keys.

But he encouraged me.

And I finally learned it.

And then CJ heard me play it and complimented my ability.

And even though I was a senior in high school and it seemed a little late in the game to be learning how to sing and play the piano, their encouragement opened up a whole new side of me.

Now I'm the dude writing a musical.

Now I'm the dude looking for a place on Broadway to perform it.

You never know what your one little encouraging comment might do for someone.

When Kristin Took Off

Kristin and I did not make our relationship public on social media for four months after we were official. I had a large young female audience, and Kristin and I were both nervous about how everyone would react. Finally, I introduced her to my fans on social media, and everyone immediately loved her. For about a year, Kristin was just Marcus Johns's girlfriend. She didn't pursue a career in social media and would only on occasion show up in my posts.

After about a year of navigating a long-distance relationship, I finally made a Q and A YouTube video with her in which I said, "Okay now, you're all going to go over and subscribe to Kristin's YouTube channel."

She thought I was joking when I filmed it, that I'd edit that part out, but I was serious. I knew she would be a successful YouTuber if she did it. I had tried for the longest time to convince her to start her own channel, but she always gave me the same answer.

"No, no. I can't do that."

"You have to do it!" I insisted, but she never wanted to pull the trigger.

So I put her on the spot in the video. I pushed her out of her comfort zone.

After that announcement on my video (which I did include, even though she thought I was just joking), she got more than twenty thousand followers. In one day.

I wish I could take credit for her success, but she built her channel to more than six hundred thousand followers and totally eclipsed my YouTube following! She did that on her own, with her own talent and skill and personality, and now she is the one who is encouraging me to post!

These days, I'm not Marcus Johns, the famous Viner/YouTuber; I'm Kristin's husband. And I wouldn't have it any other way.

That is the power of encouragement.

Even if, in that case, encouragement included a little bit of an uncomfortable push.

But hey, sometimes encouragement means pushing people out of their comfort zones and into new territory! Sometimes they're not going to get to that next level unless you keep telling them they can do it. It's easy for people to think, *It's not my turn*, or *This won't work out*, or *I'm not good enough to be able to do that*. But look at Kristin now!

She's someone people look up to, someone people go to for advice.

Every time I watch one of her videos, I think, *I wish I could be more like her.* Her consistency, hard work, and willingness to not compromise her beliefs throughout her rise have been inspiring.

Praise versus Encouragement (and the One You Shouldn't Do)

Encouragement has to be one of the most underestimated powers we have—and it's free! Absolutely free. Free to give, and free to receive—and I have no idea why we're not all out there just encouraging people left and right. Encouragement is a force, and even the smallest bit of it has the potential to change someone's life, move them in a new direction, or give them the confidence they need to keep going.

But praise? As it turns out, not so much.

Research by a Stanford professor, Dr. Carol Dweck, dives into the difference between praise and encouragement and how they impact people, especially children. It turns out that when kids are given a ton of praise, it doesn't actually motivate them to take risks—instead they become addicted to the praise and gravitate toward easier tasks just to make sure they keep getting praised. But when encouraging language is used, the kids are more willing to choose increasingly difficult tasks.

Whoa!

An article titled "Encouragement vs Praise" says, "Praise is like candy. A little can be very satisfying. Too much can cause problems. Awareness is the key. Notice if your kids are becoming addicted to praise—need it all the time."[17]

Talk about getting at the root of being willing to fail.

What if we're afraid to fail because we're addicted to praise and can't imagine making choices that might lead to a lack of praise?

I see this play out all the time in the social media world. As smaller creators, people find their content; they connect with their authenticity and talent. They become motivated to post more and grow like crazy as a result. Then somewhere along the way, they become stagnant in their development or creativity.

And it stems from the addiction to the praise. The likes. The views. The analytics. They find the one thing that works and exploit it for all its worth, because they know it will work. They just chase that dopamine hit for when their video "performs." They lose the adventure of creating new or original content, and sacrifice it for streamlining their workflow and surrounding themselves with yes-men, not *encouraging* men. It becomes nothing more than a job, and they fall out of love with this thing that used to be their passion. Their audience can't articulate it, but something has changed, something doesn't feel right.

The audience falls out of love.

And the whole ship sinks.

What if consistently encouraging those around us, instead of simply praising them for how awesome we think they are, would motivate them to take risks and try things they've never tried before? I believe this is the key to continually falling in love with life. In your job, with your hobbies, in your relationships. Keeping things new and fresh by trying new things and continually challenging your perspective with the help of encouragement from friends around you.

Four Ways to Be an Encourager

1. Keep your eyes on those close to you. I have a younger cousin named Ian. He's nineteen years old, and he probably doesn't even realize this, but whenever he encourages me about my videos, it means a lot to me. He'll shoot me a text: "Bro, that last video was your best to date. Keep it up." And it always makes me feel awesome.

The thing is, sometimes it's the encouragement of a few people close to us that means the most—not necessarily the praise of the masses. So keep your eyes open and pay attention to your friends and family, the ones who are right there with you, and be ready to encourage them. A timely word from you that encourages them in their work may be exactly what they need.

2. Be present. I know what some of you are thinking. I know what's going through your mind as I'm talking about heaping on the encouragement.

But encouraging other people makes me uncomfortable.

I don't know what to say.

What if I say something encouraging and they shrug me off?

Well, for those of you who are uncomfortable speaking your encouragement, you can encourage someone simply with your presence. On opening night of the musical, one of the most encouraging things for me was looking out into the crowd and seeing so many of my friends and family. Just having them there was a massive encouragement.

There are times when all you have to do is be present, and your presence will be the encouragement someone needs.

3. Be aware of when the stakes are high. We can use encouragement all the time, but I think we're especially in need of it when the stakes are high—you know, when you're trying something for the first time, or you reach a new level in what you're doing. I'm thinking of grand openings, opening nights, or milestones. When you see someone around you going through those kinds of things, they're ripe for encouragement. And they may need that extra little push to get them over the hump and into the next phase of whatever it is they're doing.

4. Notice others' interests and take action. People are constantly telling you what they wish for all the time. They communicate their goals, dreams, and hopes constantly. But many times, we don't hear them reaching out or expressing themselves, even when it's plain as day. A perfect example is people who say, "I wish I could play the piano." I can't tell you how many times people will come into our house, see our piano, and say, "Ah, I wish I could play."

Many of us just whiz by that type of comment and think it's nothing more than a "conversation starter." We continue on and say something like, "Oh yeah, I've been playing for five years," or "Yeah, I had lessons when I was younger," and the conversation just moves along.

But you can take these opportunities to encourage and teach—especially if you have the knowledge. It's totally free to give! Every time I hear someone say that, I say, "It's easy. I'll teach you right now." I make them sit at the piano bench as they laugh and think I'm joking, and in a few minutes, I will teach them how to play. Of course, they're not going to be Mozart in five minutes, but I can teach them four chords and say, "Look, now you can play thousands of your favorite songs!" A lot of times, taking a small fleeting moment to truly hear a desire can unlock a whole creative side of someone they never knew they had.

A lot of people wish they were doing this or knew how to do that. Many of them think they've missed their chance. They think they're too old to learn that skill. They couldn't possibly have *that* type of life. And many times, it's because no one ever told them that they could. No one ever said, "Here, sit down. I'll teach you."

You have the power to change people's minds.

You have the power to change people's opinions of themselves.

That is my favorite thing to do.

How to Find a Great Mentor (Hint: You Can't)

My subheadings are just full of encouragement today, aren't they?

Look, mentors are important. In fact, they can be crucial, especially when it comes to being a force of encouragement in your life. A mentor can open doors for you that you never could have opened on your own. They can help you see things about yourself you never would have seen without their help. They can help you explore next steps and encourage you to take risks that other people might not be too crazy about.

Mentors are, in short, amazing.

Someone recently asked me what I'd recommend they do if they want to seek out a mentor.

Finding a mentor can be extremely difficult.

It has to be someone who really identifies with you, someone who sees themselves in you.

It has to be someone who has the time to invest, along with the willingness to do it.

So, how do you go about finding a mentor?

Well, my answer is this: I wouldn't.

A mentor has to find you.

Your job is to pursue your passion, ask questions, be curious, and do the work. If you do those things, along the way you'll cross paths with someone who will see themselves in you, someone intrigued by what you're doing, someone who wants to encourage you in whatever way they can.

Mentorship is kind of like grace. Worthwhile mentors do what they do, not because they need to and not because they're making money from it; they do it because they want to help. They want to give freely. The best mentors have a track record of success, sure, but even more importantly, the best mentors aren't in it to flex their fame and get credit for helping you. The best mentors are humble, and the fact that they're walking with you through life isn't something they have to put on a résumé.

Meeting Katherine outside of her theater is a perfect example of a kind of mini-mentorship. She saw herself in me, was thrilled that I was trying to make my own opportunity, and came alongside me to help out however she could.

She didn't need to do that for free.

That's what the beginning of a mentorship looks like.

A pursuit of a passion.

A chance encounter.

And a mentor relating to you as their once younger self.

Change a Life

My entire life was changed when someone heard me singing and playing the piano.

I was stumbling around the keys, singing Michael Bublé,

and CJ Wetzler walked in and said, "Whoa! You sound amazing, man. You should sing more often."

That's it. That's all he said.

You know what? I probably didn't sound good at all. I remember in that moment I was embarrassed that he had even heard me. But that little comment of his gave me the confidence to think, *Hey, maybe I can sing!*

That changed the trajectory of my whole life.

Instead of learning one song on the piano ten years ago and quitting, I kept at it.

And now I'm the guy who wrote a musical.

Now it's your turn.

Go be the person who changes someone else's life. All it takes is a few words of encouragement.

After I put on the musical, every time I looked in the mirror, I was confronted with this huge question:

What next?

Even though it went great, even though it was a huge success, I still didn't have the feeling that it was over, that I had done everything with it that I could do. As the days passed, I realized that I really wanted to take *Viral* to the next level in the theater world.

There weren't a lot of musical theatre producers there in the audience—we had a great turnout, and we had some people in the movie industry who saw it and loved it, but the more we looked into it, the more I could tell that if I wanted to push *Viral* further, we would have to contact people in New York.

CHAPTER 12

Manifesting

We just didn't have contacts in Los Angeles with the kind of people who put on Broadway shows. We had a few small regional offers, and other people hinting at things they'd like to do with *Viral* in terms of a short series or possible film adaptation, but that's not what I wanted.

I wanted to go all the way.

I wanted *Viral* to be at the center of the musical world.

That meant New York City.

Broadway.

The more people we talked with, the more we started

hearing about the importance of doing a reading in New York. The idea is that you do a read-through of the script and host all these professionals to come and see it. This is what led us to those theaters I told you about in the last chapter. So one of my fellow producers, Lily, started putting together a team, and we set our sights on NYC.

We started talking on the phone with a New York casting director, and at first, we thought we could pull it off by October. Then we got Marc Bruni, a well-known Broadway director, interested to help direct the reading. Things were starting to really take shape. With our proposed dates of only two months away, Marc suggested we take more time, work on some rewrites, and attack it later in December. My team and I thought about it, and we realized this would be wise. However I was still itching to get to New York. To just do it. To go and meet the whole team in person and be on the ground in New York during the original dates I had wanted to be there. So I decided to fly there in October—to meet the people face-to-face, to sit in a room with them and go over every musical score, every song lyric, and talk about the show and make the changes in the flesh.

So I booked my ticket and flew to New York with Lily.

I was going to New York City.

Broadway or bust.

What Is Manifesting Anyway?

There are three main stages to any endeavor, or at least that's how I see it.

1. There is the visualizing stage. This is the stage where you do research and spend hours thinking about it, dreaming about it, wondering how it might go, and wishing it'd be amazing. So much of any creative project takes place long before the actual creation—it's the unseen part of the iceberg, the phase that so many people don't consider.

Before you do anything that will be even remotely successful, you have to imagine it. You have to envision it.

This comes really easy for me. I know a lot of people have trouble imagining themselves doing something. Maybe that's you. Maybe you don't set goals anymore because you don't think you can accomplish them. Maybe you don't even let yourself imagine amazing things.

I want to challenge you to let yourself dream again.

I have a weird set of wires in my brain that got crossed at some point—I have this belief that I can do just about anything I can imagine. Every time. It can be kind of annoying because there are usually about a thousand things I'm imagining and wanting to try, and inevitably a few of them get in the way of my ability to pursue all of them, so sometimes it's hard for me to choose or decide what to focus on.

Should I write a book or make a musical or create a documentary or film a video series with Kristin or put together a race across the country or hop on a train or learn to paraglide or start a gumball machine business or buy a property or fix up an old truck?

You get the point.

But I really believe anything is possible.

What if you gave yourself permission to think that way for just a few minutes?

What would you dream about if you thought anything was possible?

2. The second part to any endeavor is planning. This is not my strength. I'm usually ready to just jump into whatever it is that I've envisioned, and I figure I'll make it work as I go along. But all the things I've done that have turned out really great have one thing in common: they were things I spent a lot of time planning.

That's what makes or breaks any great vision, any compelling idea: planning.

Have you heard of Alex Honnold? He's one of the most famous rock climbers in the world, and the first person to free-solo El Capitan in Yosemite National Park, a three-thousand-foot rock formation.

When I say he climbed it free-solo, that means he did it without ropes.

Three thousand feet.

Did I mention he didn't have any ropes, that any misstep meant certain death?

Before he free-soloed El Cap, he made the same attempt on Half Dome, a two-thousand-foot formation. But the difference between how he approached Half Dome and how he approached El Cap is so interesting, especially with how planning relates to manifesting.

For Half Dome, he didn't prepare. He basically decided he would go there and "have an adventure." He climbed it with ropes two days before the free climb so he could get a feel for it. But on the day of his climb, he made a last-minute decision to take a different route. That took him close to the summit and back to his normal path, but it left him feeling rattled and on edge.

Near the top of Half Dome, when he could hear tourists laughing and talking at the summit (they had hiked up the back side), he panicked. He didn't trust the next foothold. He waited there, not knowing what to do. He truly believed he was about to die.

Eventually, he committed to making that step, and he made it to the top.

When he noted the climb in his journal that night, he wrote, "Do better?" with a frowny face.

He had just finished one of the greatest accomplishments of his life, but he still felt like he had let himself down.

"Do better?"

For seven years, he thought about free-soloing El Capitan, but he wanted to do this one differently. He began to visualize the climb, every single one of the thousands of holds and moves it would take to get him to the top. He stretched for a year ahead of time, gaining flexibility for one of the tough moves. He climbed the face dozens of times with ropes, rehearsing everything.

When he free-soloed El Cap, he felt nothing but exhilaration and accomplishment. He was able to enjoy the sounds of birds flying around him. At the top "it felt like mastery."[18]

So, what was the difference?

Planning.

It was the planning that defined the difference between the two climbs. It was the planning that gave him a higher level of confidence and, even more importantly, allowed him to enjoy the climb.

Once you can envision yourself doing this thing you want to do, make sure you take the time to plan.

3. After all of the planning, finally, comes the manifesting. And if you've taken some time to dream and come up with a vision for what you want to do, if you've planned and researched and prepared yourself for what's to come, manifesting comes naturally.

Manifesting is when you go out and do it.

The definition of manifest is this: "clear or obvious to the eye or mind; show (a quality or feeling) by one's acts or appearance; demonstrate."[19]

When you manifest, you are simply showing by your actions what's been clear to you for so long.

Manifesting is when I jumped on that very first train with my friends, when I plinked out that first song for the musical, when I sat my butt down and wrote the first hundred words in this book.

It all seemed like something that always existed somewhere but had never actually happened before.

Manifesting is when all of those mostly invisible things—the dreaming and the planning—become visible.

But this is also where a lot of people get lost along the way. They get cold feet. They suddenly think, *I can't do it.*

If this is you, don't stop after the dreaming and the planning. You have to follow through! If you've put in the hard work up front, no one can stop you.

That's when it's time.

It's your shot, and you have to take it.

When I traveled to New York, that was me basically saying, "I'm tired of just visualizing the next step for my musical. I'm tired of all this visualizing. Hoping, dreaming, planning. It's time. I'm just buying a ticket to fly to New York, and I'm going to meet everyone in person, and we're going to manifest this thing into existence."

When you are ready to manifest, you're telling everyone else that you're serious. You're here to make things happen, and you're not to be taken lightly.

Not Feeling Manifest-y? Try This

Manifesting is one of those things that you will often hesitate to do. It would have been much easier to just sit in my comfy house and make a few calls to prep before December. Part of me didn't want to get on a plane and leave my wife and home to go across the country to New York.

But sometimes you have to just commit and spend the money. Take the leap of faith.

So, how do you get to that point to take the leap?

I've been doing some research on energy levels, willpower, and what it takes to make up your mind and do something.

Want to get something done?

Want to stop petering out and become a manifestor of big things?

Here are a few things that may help.

Take a cold shower. Taking a cold shower when you wake up is probably the last thing you want to do in the morning, but then when you do it, you prove to yourself in the realest of ways that you have complete control over yourself and your actions.

It may sound kinda stupid, but when you turn that shower dial all the way to freezing and get under there, you decide for the rest of the day what kind of day it's going to be. It's the opposite of cheating during your diet or fast. It's kicking your self-control into high gear.

Can I run a mile today?

Well, maybe, but I have a lot to do and this and that and . . .

All of those thoughts get interrupted by the powerful, inarguable jet of cold water, and suddenly you're like, *Dang, I'm on a roll. I can do anything today!*

But don't just take it from me. A lot of people are weighing in on the benefits of cold showers, which include:[20]

- *Increased alertness*. Cold showers have all kinds of different effects on the body, including increased heart rate, higher blood pressure, and an elevated respiratory rate. All of this combines to increase the body's metabolism.
- *Stronger immune system*. "A study in the journal *PLoS One* found that people who take cold showers are 29% less likely to call in sick for work or school."[21] Studies have shown that cold water triggers the body's immune response. Or maybe people who have the fortitude to take the cold shower are just the type of people who won't call in sick for something bogus. Either way—results!
- *Boosted mood*. Some studies have suggested that because one of the body's responses to cold water is to activate the sympathetic nervous system and increase neurotransmitters, people may be less likely to experience depressive symptoms directly following a cold shower.
- *Reduced pain*. Restricted blood vessels help reduce swelling and edema that cause pain.

So if you're having trouble getting motivated to manifest, try starting your days with cold showers!

Small victories. Maybe the last thing in the world you're going to do in the morning is take a cold shower. Fine. I still think you should consider it, but if cold showers are off the table, think of a way you can start off with a victory. Maybe that means going to the gym or eating a healthy breakfast or waking up early.

What's something you can do in the morning that will

give you positive vibes? Something that will make you feel like you're on the right track? Something that can become part of your daily routine and make it easier for you to manifest that day's work.

We all need something to jump-start our day! For most people that's coffee, but come on. That's a crutch at best, a drug at worst, and are you most people? I say cold showers, but any small victory that gives you the feeling of being on a roll will work just fine.

Make a list. Every single thing in this book is advice I stand by.

Now that doesn't mean I follow it all the time. Ha!

But if I were to give myself tips, or try to get back on the right track after having fallen off it, these are all things I would do.

Making lists is one of these things.

If you're feeling unable to manifest the big, challenging things in your life, one way to get things going is to make a list, and when I say make a list, I mean include even the most mundane things. Like "brush your teeth." And then, after you brush your teeth, mark it off. There's something wonderful about lists, about seeing the increased number of things you are marking off and completing.

Making a list not only validates all the small things you're doing, but it also helps you realize just how important and valuable your time is. As you look at the new list of things to do that you've created, think about how long each of these things will take. If you wrote down "eat breakfast," think about how long it will take you to do it and the percentage of your day it will take up, and be aware of how much time you'll need to get through your entire list.

Making lists is a huge step toward manifesting.

Schedule free time. While you're making your list, don't forget one of the most important items to add: free time. Schedule it into your day. What do you like to do?

Play video games?

Read?

Listen to music?

Play on your phone?

Video chat with your friends?

Put it on your schedule! Give your mind time to relax. And have fun! If your entire life is nothing but checking unfun things off your list, your ability to manifest your goals and dreams will plummet. Besides, it's just plain miserable.

Schedule fun things into your life and you'll be at total peace when you're being a little lazy here and there. Cause, hey, from five to nine, you scheduled lazy time!

Don't Cut It Down

Right in the middle of writing this book, I had a really bad day. Not just a day when you wake up feeling off, but the kind of day where thing after thing after thing goes wrong, and you start to wonder what's wrong with you, why things aren't working out—and before you know it, you're in a pit of despair.

I'm talking about a really bad day.

Ever have one of those?

It all started with an online auction for a property I had spent a lot of time researching. I was excited about it, pretty pumped about the plans I was putting together in my head, and then, out of nowhere, I got outbid. It was like a gut punch.

Oof.

That was the first thing that told me the day was going to be a bad one. And on a regular day, if that was the only thing, I probably could have brushed it off. But there was also the constant friction of seeing my musical take too long to get off the ground, along with the deadlines associated with writing this book. The feelings of letting people down in various areas of my life, and then getting feedback on *Viral* and discovering that I'd have to rewrite almost the entire play because the changes being asked for would reverberate throughout the entire script.

The entire thing.

Oh, man. I was so overwhelmed.

Underneath it all was the mounting pressure to make something of *Viral*, and a fear that nothing would come of it, after I had spent two years of my life on it. What if the whole musical just faded away? How can I justify all the time and energy I put into it?

This was quickly followed by all of these bizarre "You can't do it" thoughts that began buzzing through my mind.

You don't know anyone in New York.

You're at the total mercy of everyone planning this thing.

Do you realize how much this showcase is going to cost?

I turned to my YouTube channel for some encouragement. Maybe I could find a few small successes there to celebrate—I just wanted to turn this day around. Two videos I had put together were doing really well, which was great, but then the most recent two, which were a little more niche, tanked. I stared at the viewer numbers on the screen.

Could that be right?

That started getting in my head too.

Are my instincts totally gone?

Am I heading in the right direction?

What am I doing?

I was so upset. So upset. I felt like I was literally at the end of my energy, the end of my will.

I had no desire to manifest anything. But that's when this intriguing idea snuck into my mind. I decided to take a video of myself talking through all these issues. I don't even know where this came from.

Okay, I thought, *I'm going to just pull out my camera and talk.*

I started recording the video, and I just sat there, didn't even open my mouth or say anything.

I didn't think I had the words to express how down I was, nor even the energy to move my lips. I had zero desire to manifest anything—except maybe going to bed and sleeping for a week straight. I literally stared at the camera for five minutes as it just kept rolling.

Finally, the words came out. And I told the camera what I was seeing in my head. I didn't know what else to say. All I had was an image of an old tree in my mind. And I don't usually do this—in fact, I don't know if I've ever done it before—but I just focused on that image and dove down into the deepest parts of my brain, the abstract parts, and I asked myself what I was really seeing. And this is what I saw.

I saw a very old tree. Like a giant willow tree, gnarled and weathered looking. Very rustic. It stood by itself, with nothing green on it anymore. It had no leaves because of the season it was in, and I knew that, but I suddenly envisioned just chopping it down. And for a moment I enjoyed that idea, the sensation of the axe digging into the trunk, me killing the tree, even though I knew the only reason it wasn't green was because of the season.

My brain kicked in and said, "You're feeling bad because *Viral* isn't producing the fruit you want, but this is an old, wise, beautiful tree, and you shouldn't give up on it or cut it down just because it's winter. You need winter in order to get to spring, to get to summer, to get to fall. This is the part of the cycle you're in."

And in the vision I had in my brain, I stepped back and looked around.

There were other trees all around my old tree, and they were growing fast. Taller and taller. These trees were growing so quickly and taking in all the surrounding light, which meant my tree wasn't getting the sunlight it needed. And the thing about those other trees was that they were all so generic. They were all the same.

I thought to myself, *Will anyone notice my tree? Or will people forget about its uniqueness?*

At the end, I came to a strong conclusion: *My old tree is valuable. It's not something I should cut down.*

I talked about all of this on camera, and sometimes it really helps to articulate how you're feeling, what you're thinking, what you're hoping for. In the process, I had the chance to look at myself and my situation from another, outside perspective.

Of course, the tree is valuable.

Of course, there's no point in cutting it down.

In fact, if I were to see someone cut down a tree like that in a movie, it would be horrible, almost obscene.

I was able to understand myself and how I was feeling on a deeper level. After I finished recording the video, I was upset for a little bit, and I cried for a little bit, and then I got back into the rest of my day.

And you know what?

The next day, I moved ahead.

The next day, I was able to manifest.

I buzzed through a few more chapters for this book. I made a few more plans for *Viral*'s showcase.

And I thought to myself, *You just wait until everyone gets to see what you're actually capable of.*

Don't underestimate the power of recovering your optimism—that's the source of your power! Regardless of outcomes, failure, or wild success, your optimism will keep you going on that next big thing.

That inner voice that knows you have something unbelievable to contribute—something that everyone needs? That voice is everything, and you need to listen to it in you. It's there, but sometimes you have to call it out, or listen hard to it. Sometimes what brings out that optimistic voice in yourself is when you commit to calling it out of others.

Encourage.

Teach.

Give opportunities to others.

That's how it works. This contagious manifesting really can save the world.

It's not hocus-pocus.

It's not a pipe dream.

And it's even more powerful than any luck or hard work . . . or cold shower.

You've got this.

You can do it.

Epilogue

Well, here we are.

The end.

And I guess it would be awesome if I were to send you out into the world by reiterating that you can do it!

You can do anything you set your mind to!

Yeah . . . about that.

You know how you can get those high-pitched ringing noises in your head? When I was younger, my brother told me that those sounds in your ear happened when you lost a tiny sensory hair in your ear. And whatever that pitch was that you heard, that was the last time you would hear that specific pitch as it slowly faded away into silence.

Good old Cody. He told me all kinds of stuff.

This idea horrified me. But when I was young, I had never had that experience, or at least never took notice of it. Besides, I honestly didn't know if it was true, or even verifiable.

But that story my brother told me has stuck with me for all these years.

I even remember everyone in my family taking a test on YouTube that played a high frequency noise that slowly got lower. It would begin with a light, high, tinny noise and eventually turn into a louder and more obvious, deep ring. As predicted, my parents couldn't hear the mosquito-buzzing higher frequency.

But I always could, as could my siblings.

Years later, we did the same test with a cousin of mine who is about eight years younger than I am. It was a good old throwback challenge to see if we had the same hearing abilities that we had years before.

Sure enough, my cousin Ian winced at the sound of the high pitch frequency.

But this time my experience was different, because while he could obviously hear that pitch, my siblings and I looked around in silence.

We thought he was joking at first, but it was true: we didn't have the same hearing ability as our younger teenage cousin.

Eventually we heard the noise, and only much later could my parents begin to hear a lower frequency noise. About which we all made fun of them.

"At least we're not *that* deaf," we said, laughing.

But all joking aside, this really hit me hard.

I am getting *old*.

I mean, I know I'm only twenty-six, but my body cannot do what it once physically could (even if those differences are still barely recognizable).

After we took that test the second time with my cousin, I started paying attention to any ringing noise I heard.

In the last year, I noticed something strange and slightly alarming: I was hearing this ringing more and more frequently.

I started to get nervous about it. Was I losing my hearing? I always thought my brother's explanation was nothing more than an old wives' tale.

But.

Could there be a correlation between my suddenly

hearing these ringing noises in my ears and the fact that I had lost my ability to hear those high frequency sounds?

It must be proof! I thought.

I started hearing that noise a lot at night when everything in the house was quiet. Lying there in bed, I listened as the noise faded in and then out, and I thought to myself, *There it goes. I'll never hear that particular pitch again. I'm going deaf. I'm getting old.*

Seriously. Hearing these tones and wondering if this was the last time I would ever hear them had me thinking a lot about mortality in a strange way.

The end of me.

Then a couple gray hairs came in on the sides of my head.

That was it.

I was slowly dying.

Not growing anymore, but dying. Declining. Decaying.

And for the first time in my life, I was face-to-face with something I literally could not do anything about.

You can try to stop the aging process.

You can try to keep yourself from looking older.

But guess what?

You can't do it.

You can't stop it.

Wait, I thought. *Maybe I can slow death.*

Maybe I can.

I scoured the web, did all kinds of research, read every article I could find on health, pills, vitamins, special shampoos.

More research.

Wait . . . Six months before I see signs of reversal?

Aargh!

More stress, which probably gave me more gray hairs.

I was paranoid and became intensely aware of every single sign of decay, every sign that my body was getting older, breaking down, heading toward death.

Hmmm.

My teeth are getting worse.

Maybe soon I'll even have those nasty yellow toenails.

I'm going to overcome this! I'm not going to get older.

But you know what?

It's impossible. We all get old. And start to slow down. And for a control freak, an even scarier thought echoed in the back of my brain: *There's nothing I can do to stop it.*

And it's true, you can't get younger. You can't. I can't do it. For real.

What does that mean for me? What does it mean for my future?

Jeez, if I feel old, just think about Mom and Dad and how they feel about all this.

I found myself thinking about life, about my family, about Kristin. And it hit me—my life is moving so, so fast. I had this glimpse of understanding, a quick revelation that time flies.

Time flies.

It really does. I know it because it was happening to me.

I called my dad, and we chatted for a while. First, some small talk.

"How's the house?"

"Retirement is just around the corner, huh? How's that feel?"

And then our conversation spun in a different direction, and he started telling me about how his aunts and uncles could barely walk.

"It's so strange and sad to see them joke about dying,"

he said, and there was a strange sound in my dad's voice. "If you think life moves fast now, Marcus, the next thirty years of your life will go ten times faster."

It hit me hard, listening to my dad joke about how he was next in line for the wheelchair, the retirement home. It was strange to think about his aunts and uncles joking about the next stage.

Death.

My mind raced.

"Oh, yeah," I said, coming back to the present. "I love you, Dad."

"I love you too, Marcus," he said.

"Bye."

I need to call my dad more.

All I can think right now is, *We are but a vapor.*

I pray, "God give me peace about this." And believe it or not, at that exact moment a slight ring starts to sound in my ears.

But this time I feel different. This time I smile, take a deep breath, let it out.

God, you are in control.

I am okay. Dad is okay.

Everything I can't do, God can. I am not going to worry. Instead of wanting to hold on to that ringing sound in a sad attempt to preserve that tone in my head, I let it go. I give all of my worries and concerns about aging and hearing and life to God. And I say a prayer as the sound fades away.

"God, thank you for allowing me to hear that. Thanks for all the time I've gotten with that specific sound. With my dad. With my life."

It seems funny to me, how only God can turn something that is a triggering point of anxiety into a sign for me to know that God is speaking. Speaking specifically to me, reminding me to be thankful for the time I have had and the time I have to come.

Now, when I hear a ringing in my ears, I hear God. I feel a sense of perspective.

Don't let the fear control you—cast it onto Jesus, and he will take care of it.

I can't control it if I lose some silly ability to hear high pitch frequencies, or if I go completely deaf or gray. I can't control how soon I will die.

But I can control my choices, and that helps change my perspective.

I choose to believe God is in control.

And when I can't do it, he can.

Acknowledgments

They told me to write an acknowledgments section for the end of the book. Who are "they," you ask? Well, that's exactly what this part is for.

If it weren't for Zondervan, I wouldn't even know about an acknowledgments section. Which perfectly describes why I think you were crazy for giving me a chance to write a book. So much gratitude to the whole team, especially Tom, Mick, and Shawn.

To my team—Clayton, Team Scale, CAA, and Anthony—thank you for telling me that I could do it.

To my wife, Kristin—you are lying in bed next to me as I write right now. Just your presence alone is what keeps me going. Gives me peace. And keeps me focused. The one who rolls over and says, "Hey, you're not writing, Mister!" in a sweet and reminding way to keep me on track when I go down a YouTube rabbit hole. What would I do without you?

To my brothers and sisters—Cody, Lexy, Shelby, and Nate. It all means nothing if we don't have each other. My greatest support team and inner circle. I won't make a move if you all don't approve.

Mom and Dad—I'm indebted. You make me want to be

the most intentionally loving and caring parent to pay it forward. You have given me a wonderful life and a God-centered worldview. What more of a gift could one person receive?

To all the Toinks—you know who you are. Love you guys. There's too many to list.

Andy Pagana—you'll never know how far your encouragement has brought me.

And finally, Jesus Christ. My Lord and Savior. Thank you. I pray you use this book in some small way to be a light in this world.

Notes

1. Cited in Tim Mulligan, "What the Death of Vine Means for Super Short Form Video," MIDIA, October 28, 2016, www.midiaresearch.com/blog/what-the-death-of-vine-means-for-super-short-form-video.
2. Quoted in Pranav, "Dealing with Rejections: Career Lessons from Super Bowl Champion Tom Brady," Medium, February 5, 2019, https://medium.com/@pranavnaik_94761/dealing-with-rejections-career-lessons-from-super-bowl-champion-tom-brady-b85ee599418d.
3. Cited in "Tom Brady: Football Player (1977–)," Biography, April 15, 2019, www.biography.com/athlete/tom-brady.
4. See Cork Gaines, "Tom Brady Considered Transferring in College but Instead Accepted the Challenge of Getting Better and Becoming the Starter," Business Insider, February 3, 2019, www.businessinsider.com/tom-brady-michigan-transfer-cal-depth-chart-starter-2019-2.
5. "Jim Carrey: Biography," IMDb, www.imdb.com/name/nm0000120/bio?ref_=nm_ov_bio_sm.
6. Quoted in Benjamin Svetkey, "Jim Carrey's Serious Turn in *The Truman Show*," *Entertainment*, June 5, 1998, https://ew.com/article/1998/06/05/jim-carreys-serious-turn-truman-show.
7. See John Forster, *The Life and Times of Oliver Goldsmith*, vol. 1 (Leipzig: Bernhard Tauchnitz, 1873), 207.

8. See "Trust Your Gut," YouTube, March 18, 2016, https://www.youtube.com/watch?v=fu7HfZulm2M.
9. Al Pittampalli, "When Should You Trust Your Gut? Here's What the Science Says," November 16, 2017, www.psychologytoday.com/us/blog/are-you-persuadable/201711/when-should-you-trust-your-gut-heres-what-the-science-says.
10. See Pittampalli, "When Should You Trust Your Gut?"
11. See Cari Nierenberg, "The Science of Intuition: How to Measure 'Hunches' and 'Gut Feelings,'" Live Science, May 20, 2016, www.livescience.com/54825-scientists-measure-intuition.html.
12. See Galang Lufityanto, Chris Donkin, and Joel Pearson, "Measuring Intuition: Nonconscious Emotional Information Boosts Decision Accuracy and Confidence," *Psychological Science*, April 6, 2016, 1–13, www.researchgate.net/publication/304538511_Measuring_intuition_Nonconscious_emotional_information_boosts_decision_accuracy_and_confidence.
13. See Jessica Stillman, "Science: Your Anxiety Is Killing Your Intuition," *Inc.*, October 25, 2017, www.inc.com/jessica-stillman/science-stress-silences-your-gut-instincts.html.
14. "Imposter syndrome," Dictionary.com, www.dictionary.com/browse/impostor-syndrome.
15. P. T. Barnum, *Art of Money Getting* (Bedford, MA: Applewood, 1999), 43.
16. Gary Vaynerchuk, *Crushing It!* (New York: HarperBusiness, 2018), 60.
17. "Encouragement vs Praise," Positive Discipline, www.positivediscipline.com/articles/encouragement-vs-praise.
18. Alex Honnald, "How I Climbed a 3,000-Foot Vertical Cliff—without Ropes," TED 2018, April 2018, www.ted

.com/talks/alex_honnold_how_i_climbed_a_3_000_foot_vertical_cliff_without_ropes/up-next.

19. "Manifest," *Lexico*, www.lexico.com/definition/manifest.
20. See Rachel Nall, "Are There Any Health Benefits to Cold Showers?" *Medical News Today*, July 11, 2019, www.medicalnewstoday.com/articles/325725.php#stronger-immune-system.
21. Quoted in Nall, "Are There Any Health Benefits to Cold Showers?"